KEEPING HOPE ALIVE

THE HARPER & ROW SERIES ON THE PROFESSIONS

KEEPING
HOPE
ALIVE

On Becoming a Psychotherapist

F. Robert Rodman, M.D.

Foreword by Robert Coles

HARPER & ROW, PUBLISHERS, New York
Cambridge, Philadelphia, San Francisco, London
Mexico City, São Paulo, Singapore, Sydney

Grateful acknowledgment is made for permission to reprint:

"To the One of Fictive Music" from *Collected Poems of Wallace Stevens* by Wallace Stevens. Copyright 1923 by Wallace Stevens; copyright renewed 1951 by Wallace Stevens. Reprinted by permission of Alfred A. Knopf, Inc.

Excerpt from "New Introductory Lectures on Psychoanalysis" from *The Standard Edition of the Complete Psychological Works of Sigmund Freud*, translated and edited by James Strachey. Copyright © 1964, 1965 by James Strachey. Reprinted by permission of W. W. Norton & Company, Inc., Sigmund Freud Copyrights, The Institute of Psycho-Analysis, and The Hogarth Press.

FIRST EDITION

Designer: Sidney Feinberg

Library of Congress Cataloging-in-Publication Data

Rodman, F. Robert (Francis Robert), date
  Keeping hope alive.

  (The Harper & Row series on the professions)
  Includes index.
  1. Psychotherapy—Vocational guidance. 2. Psychotherapy—Practice. 3. Psychotherapy. 4. Psychoanalysis. I. Title. II. Series.
  RC455.2.P8R63 1986   616.89'14   85-45224
  ISBN 0-06-015537-X

---

86 87 88 89 90 10 9 8 7 6 5 4 3 2 1

To Kathy

CONTENTS

ACKNOWLEDGMENTS

By disclosing their deepest feelings and thoughts, my patients have vastly enlarged the scope of my life. I have striven to be worthy of their trust. I thank them one and all.

I am grateful to Professor Knut Larsson, whose invitation to lecture at the University of Gothenburg, Sweden, called forth the material that was to become this book. Some of the conceptualizations took root in a subsequent period of supervising the child therapists of the city of Gothenburg. I thank Birgitta Steg, who coordinated and supported that work for several years.

My old and cherished friends Ulf and Birgitta Larsson taught me the meaning of the phrase "good enough." I am grateful to them for that, and for so much more.

Ted Solotaroff, my editor, showed extraordinary patience and skill during a long writing process. He has been a most perceptive and inspiring guide throughout.

Lance Lee, poet and playwright, contributed substantially to the organization of this book, just as he did to my earlier *Not Dying*. I am deeply grateful for the gift of his friendship and for his superb literary skills.

I thank my stalwart friend Dr. Samuel Wilson for his trenchant perspectives on the nature of our task and on the people who try to carry it out, and for his pertinent comments in the final preparation of the manuscript.

My colleagues in Group 9 at the Center for Advanced Psychoanalytic Studies, Princeton, New Jersey, have been an unfailing source of stimulation and fellowship. I thank them in particular for the high standard of their deliberations, and for demonstrating how psychoanalysts may vigorously differ without victory and defeat hanging in the balance.

My family tolerated a wide variety of moods during the extended period during which this work was written and revised. They saw me through these times with unfailing support. I love them for that and for all the incalculable rest.

FOREWORD

Throughout most of this century psychoanalysis has found America to be particularly receptive to its ideas and practice. Freud's famous lectures at Clark University in 1909 earned him the favorable notice of, among others, our greatest psychologist, William James. Even in the 1920s before the rise of Hitler brought many of its leading figures to America, psychoanalytic psychiatry was taking firm root in America's major cities—a development that Stanley Cobb, the distinguished neuropsychiatrist who taught at Harvard Medical School and worked at the Massachusetts General Hospital, explained as "a consequence of the open-minded curiosity of the American public, especially in matters of health." In 1964 the late Dr. Grete Bibring, one of the most prominent American psychoanalysts of the time (and a member of Freud's Viennese circle before her arrival in Boston), offered this explanation to me of "the climate of welcome," as she put it, that had made America the world center of Freudian psychology:

> My husband and I [her husband, Edward Bibring, also was a psychoanalyst] noted immediately how interested Americans are in psychology. In Europe we had lived a quiet life and did our research and treated patients; here, all eyes were on us

analysts—very hard to understand, at first. Now that I have been here for many years I understand some of the reasons: the emphasis on the individual—on the here-and-now, rather than on a future life of heaven or hell; and the emphasis, also, on efficiency, on each person doing the very most that is possible; and then there is the optimism here, the hope (the expectation, even) that if you will find the right person, the best person, then certain problems, at least, will be solved.

I thought of that interview I had with Dr. Bibring as I read this remarkably candid and edifying book—one that places "hope" in its title, and offers a great deal of good sense from start to finish. Dr. Rodman is Dr. Bibring's "right person"— someone whose wisdom (the result of years of dedicated, attentive, caring work with diverse patients) graces this book throughout and makes it an especially important one for understanding how America's therapists become the particular kind of professional people they are, and what their occupation offers in the way of opportunities, difficulties, satisfactions, potential hazards.

No effective therapist can afford to be at a psychological remove from himself or herself, Dr. Rodman tells us, right off. In a tactful but persistent manner he uses his personal experiences to illuminate the therapist's working life—constant attentiveness to the patient's words and manner of presentation, of course, but a corresponding willingness, also, to take oneself seriously, not in the mode of self-display or self-aggrandizement or just plain self-preoccupation, but as an important gesture of concern for those troubled human beings who have come asking, in their various ways, for assistance. The therapist's constantly scrutinized subjectivity will enable the patient, ultimately, to become more objective about what it is that has caused so much personal pain. Freud learned to keep close watch of his apparently random thoughts, his fantasies by day and his nighttime dreams—for he knew that what a patient told him had to be filtered through his own personality, his own intellect, his own memory before it could be handed back as a responsive gift to one in need of enlightened generosity: the careful, thoughtful listener's clarifying statement.

In this book a physician, a psychiatrist, a psychoanalyst tells us of his personal journey from a particular childhood in New England to a professional career in California. The essentially autobiographical nature of the first half of the book will hold the reader's full attention, because it is a narrative that is rendered exceedingly well—clear language, vivid details, effective mix of factuality and introspective commentary. I would ask the person about to read this book to consider, too, the author's courage—his ability to share, openly and compellingly, the more private aspects of what makes one choose to become a therapist. "Every analyst learned to understand the mind and heal the mind's conflicts as a child," my own analyst once told me—an observation prompted by the account I'd given of my mother, my father, my early life with them. Dr. Rodman gives us, his readers, a chance to reflect upon the earliest moments of his therapeutic career—a mother's sadness, a loving child's sense of that and his desire to be of help. Those brief moments of our early years that we remember are, of course, summary flash points, as it were—heightened condensations of days and weeks and months, thousands of experiences, worries, apprehensions, times of good spirits and times of low spirits. We are not given in the pages that follow any abstract formulations of a life's early psychology; we are not handed a family's "dynamics." But we are ever so gently yet forthrightly made to realize that the Dr. Rodman who is now such an accomplished, weathered therapist has, all along the way—through the years of his schooling, then training, then the long stretch of learning that takes place in a private office—been the person who took qualities from his mother, his father, and assembled them in a way that, eventually, made it possible for a therapist to emerge.

In our franker moments with ourselves I think all of us who practice psychotherapy remember the first experience of "becoming a psychotherapist"—whom we tried to mend or restore emotionally, from what, and how (a smile, some words, an offering of time and concern). I remember such times in my own life, and Lord, I remember seeing and hearing some of the children I've come to know do their healing—try to make things easier for one or another parent, or brother, or sister, or grandparent. In New Orleans, twenty-five years ago, I watched four terribly embattled black girls, each only six years old, struggle with mobs threatening their lives, and with a white boycott that completely emptied the schools to which they were assigned by a federal judge. I was interested as a social observer in how they managed such a severe racial crisis—managed the personal danger they faced every day. But I was also a child psychiatrist, and will never forget one of the girls, Tessie, telling me about her mother—the high blood pressure she had, the serious, impairing headaches, the spells of gloom that came upon her: "If my momma feels good before I leave, I'm ready for those people in the [heckling] mob. I tell the men [federal marshals protecting her] that I'll be fine. If my momma isn't feeling good, then I be down and want to quit the school and stay with momma and try to make her better. I want to help out with the house. I want to try to cheer her up. If she be real low, she cries, but hugging me helps, she says. I can get her to laugh!"

I share Dr. Rodman's admiration for Anna Freud, and like him, made the trek (it was almost spiritual in nature) to London, where for so many years that extraordinarily gifted and conscientious child analyst did her work and taught others to follow in her tradition. I remember telling Miss Freud about Tessie and her American struggles—and hearing her reply: "This child may be going through a lot of hardship in the South, but her mind certainly is on her mother as well as the mobs. It sounds as if she's the mother's only doctor!" The mother had no money, and it was true, no regular physician to attend her. Tessie helped her considerably. Many of us who join the so-called "helping professions" will remember such moments in our lives, and Dr. Rodman does well to nudge us toward such memories in his book.

Another important subject he discusses is the matter of how one learns to do psychotherapy—the very heart of the matter, of course. There are courses to take, books to read, journals to get to know, lists of diagnostic possibilities to learn, special lectures from visiting dignitaries to attend, supervisory instruction to arrange, and all of that helps a great deal. But factuality and "technique" (for example, when to say what to which kind of patients under which set of clinical circumstances) are not to be equated with psychotherapy, which is, really, what a particular person does with all the educational experiences just mentioned: how he or she works them into his or her mind and heart, and learns to use them, to share them with others.

If it is any comfort to the person who wants to be a psychotherapist, a similar way of looking at things is quite congenial to many of us who are the teachers, the supervisors. We, too, are constantly trying to figure out how to be of help to our students, how to teach not only a "subject matter," but a manner of being with others. We are, each of us, different in important ways, and those differences give a particular shape to our "personalities," as students learn, not to mention patients. In recent years, as I've supervised residents in child psychiatry, I've come to appreciate over and over again how *individual* each psychotherapist's education is, and how differently residents make use of a supervisory hour and even how differently they respond in a group situation to an interview with a patient, a point of theory, a professional article, or a book. They are all making an intellectual and personal journey of their own, the same kind of journey so sensitively and subtly mapped by Dr. Rodman. He dares to let us know how he kept learning even from his periods of doubt and confusion and apprehension—maybe learned most through them. That memorable phrase of Yeats, "slouching towards Bethlehem," applies to the training of psychotherapists, or one hopes it does: the humble and burdened side of the search we all make with respect to the mind's mysteries. There is no smugness or self-importance in Dr. Rodman even now, after he has become the psychotherapist he wanted to become. Indeed, one suspects that he, too, is still struggling, still trying to figure out *when, how, with whom* one says or does *this* or *that.*

Not that there aren't specifics to learn—particular matters which all of us who work with patients have to be prepared to address. The question of fees, of insurance, of where we work and with which kind of patients. This book offers important information with respect to those matters, and the would-be psychotherapist will find that information helpful indeed. But most of all, I suspect, he or she will be grateful for the person who gradually emerges in this book, a wise and kind and sensitive doctor who is relaxed enough to share with us his concerns, his worries and doubts, his defeats as well as his victories.

He also does well to acknowledge the vexing and sometimes discouraging institutional and ideological struggles which unfortunately plague the psychoanalytic movement. The "factionalism" he mentions encountering in Los Angeles a couple of decades ago was not some singular episode in psychoanalysis or psychiatry. There is something instructively humbling about the rancor, pride, and zealotry one occasionally sees in a profession which aims to offer the world insight into the causes of such behavior. To be fair, sectarian squabbling is by no means limited to people who are psychotherapists. But it can be hard—trying to "keep hope alive" in oneself as a psychological listener, and in one's patients, who need all the nurturing they can get, while protecting one's professional and intellectual life from the embittering influences generated by fiercely self-righteous arguments carried on by various "schools" or "institutes" and the ambitious theorists who often dominate them. The "therapeutic witch-hunt" which Dr. Rodman warns against as the nemesis of a psychotherapist's work can also haunt the institutions where those therapists are trained—those endless *ad hominem* assaults on anyone and everyone who doesn't adhere to the party line.

But his book is never a lamentation or a sardonic muck-raking. The author, rather, comes across as a thoroughly solid, decent, hardworking, skilled doctor whom any of us would feel lucky and privileged indeed to have as a therapist. He is also a first-rate writer of clear, accessible prose which holds the reader's interest. There is a marvelous mix of head and heart in these pages—a thoughtful, highly developed intellect that is not afraid of the emotional side of this life, the bursts of enthusiasm or the spells of gloom which descend upon us and affect us as therapists as well as friends, husbands, wives, parents. I had read his powerful, haunting first book, *Not Dying:* the close account of an anguishing personal struggle he waged over a decade ago. I had noted in it his capacity to connect his working life with the abyss fate had led him to—the death of his much loved young wife. Now he has pressed further, mobilized a narrative gift (which at times rises to the lyrical) in the service of an important educational effort—to teach those who would be therapists (and remind us who already are) what we are about, and what we ought to be about.

—ROBERT COLES

Scientific thinking does not differ in its nature from the normal activity of thought, which all of us, believers and unbelievers, employ in looking after our affairs in ordinary life. It has only developed certain features: it takes an interest in things even if they have no immediate, tangible use; it is concerned carefully to avoid individual factors and affective influences; it examines more strictly the trustworthiness of the sense-perceptions on which it bases its conclusions; it provides itself with new perceptions which cannot be obtained by everyday means and it isolates the determinants of these new experiences in experiments which are deliberately varied. Its endeavor is to arrive at correspondence with reality—that is to say, with what exists outside us and independently of us and, as experience has taught us, is decisive for the fulfillment or disappointment of our wishes. This correspondence with the real external world we call "truth."

SIGMUND FREUD
New Introductory Lectures on Psychoanalysis

Unreal, give back to us what once you gave:
The imagination that we spurned and crave.

WALLACE STEVENS
"To the One of Fictive Music"

PART I

THE TRAINING

1.

THE

OBSERVING

THERAPIST

Every patient stared at long enough, listened to hard enough, yields up a child, arrived from somewhere else, caught up in a confused life, trying to do the right thing, whatever that may be, and doing the wrong thing instead. At first, I was stunned to see this suddenly visible face of innocence. But in the course of time, I learned to recognize that when it appears, I have grasped what binds my patient and me together, our common lot, and the only reasonable basis on which a pair of human beings may proceed.

A twenty-eight-year-old man who had sought treatment with me because of difficulty in progressing as an architect was coming to the end of his two years of therapy. He had an original imagination which had begun to earn him a measure of acclaim, but he lost many potential commissions because his proposals were often somewhat impractical. His appearance was notable for the fact that his left eye turned outward. This introduced doubt about the direction of his gaze and about whether he was really listening to me. He had exploited this ambiguity of appearance throughout his life to make himself unpredictable. In therapy, this also took the form of a sudden rejection of what I was saying, always set up by repeated gestures of agreement. He could accept only a few correct statements before being threatened with a feeling of impoverishment or intimidation. But his need to undermine our sessions had gradually declined after arduous interpretive work.

He began an hour toward the end of his therapy by discussing a client who was dissatisfied with a design he had submitted. I found myself thinking of a big doll, such as I used to have in my office playroom, a sand-weighted, blown-up, child-sized doll the children could punch. Going on to tell me about his grammar school teachers, whom he used to goad in order to demonstrate what fools they were, my patient then talked about his relationship to me, and in particular those moments when he would reverse course and dispute the worth of what I had been saying. His timely grins, compounded of defiance and willful stupidity, had expressed this state perfectly. And now he smiled too, this time warmly. "What a pain I must have been," he said.

I thought of something I had read: schoolboy buffoons often act the part of the castrated. I recalled that the concept might be applied to all males who clowned around. A random bit of insight, lying unused for years in a corner of my mind, suddenly became valuable. Here was an actual person to whom it might apply.

I began to reevaluate and realign much of what I already knew, in the light of a dawning understanding which was going to take us deeper yet. He had believed that neither of his parents fostered his masculine development, and that his father, who was subservient to his mother, had particularly cheated him of support. He had begun to get a longed-for masculine feeling in therapy with me, whom he styled "mountain man," right at the beginning, in a landmark dream that incorporated a reference to a plaid shirt I wore on one occasion. I was cast as the alternative father with whom he could reenact his early conflict, and who, if therapy went well enough, would enable him to patch in the masculine development he had missed. He brought various pressures to bear on me, which showed that he was perceiving me in accordance with his childhood experience with parents, attempting to behave in resentful, subversive ways that would be congruent with such perceptions, but also idealizing me as one who could rescue him from this compulsion. I had tried most of all to make him conscious of his confusion about me, and of past and present, hoping for a process of sorting which would gradually lead to clarity.

When I told him of my impression that he felt like a defiant and castrated boy, who had aimed to emasculate the father substitutes who were his teachers, he was silent for a moment and then enthusiastically developed the idea by relating a recurrent dream from childhood. It featured a spinning disk of the sort one might see in a shooting gallery on a carnival midway, a target with the face of Richard Nixon painted on it. A low and dragging voice, which sounded like a slowed-down phonograph record of Nixon speaking, accompanied the creaky and forebodingly persistent turning of the disk. He dreamed the same dream many times. In the New England village in which he was reared, the patient, a boy during the late 1960s and early 1970s, was exposed to daily discussion of the Vietnam war on television and in family conversation. He saw in Nixon an ineffectual father, one who does not respond and is not responded to. While he talked about his dream, it occurred to me that the big doll of my imagination, which can be punished at will but is never altered by experience, is both the child's mocking version of the ineffectual father, one who sets no example of fruitful responsiveness and growth, and an accusatory symbol of what he has done to his child. It could, of course, have other meanings as well.

I told him that his sudden reversals of attitude had represented an effort to provoke me into behaving like a present-day version of Richard Nixon. But just as with the predecessor of Nixon, his own father, he was of two minds about having an ineffectual authority figure. One side of him wished to have the pleasure of triumph over a depreciated therapist, but in that case he knew he would not be able to learn what he needed to know to become an effective person himself. He also wanted me to survive these attacks and to understand them correctly so that he could make things right at last.

He shook his head as I told him the idea, and at first I thought this meant disagreement. But when he spoke I could tell that it was more a gesture of frustration with himself for not having seen this before. He was amazed that it was possible to put into words matters of such importance, unconscious until then. "It's obvious," he said. "How could I not have known it?"

His recurrent dream reminded me of an important event in my own life, an appendectomy when I was six. While the anesthetic was taking effect in spite of my struggle to break free of the smothering mask, I experienced some frightening visual imagery, including a spinning disk, a spiral that turned, however, not draggingly but more and more rapidly and fearfully until a climactic explosive noise dispelled it entirely and made way for blankness, a sense of quietude, I think, and probably a dream. This experience was the culminating trauma in the stage of life when a boy is preoccupied by castration fears from a guilty rivalry with his father. The white-coated surgeon was going to make a cut in my lower abdomen, and my father—the man behind the surgeon, so to speak—wore a white coat, too. I had often seen him wearing it in the market where he worked. The fears of this period had left their mark on my development, and had helped to determine my choice of medicine as a profession.

Knowing about spinning disks and castration fantasies associated with them, I was able to feel with my patient in his struggle to overcome a sense of being thwarted. My experience as an analytic patient had acquainted me with the importance of the appendectomy and the anesthesia experience, but I had never looked at the details of the imagery until this hour.

There is more that could be said about this interesting young man. But I think I've made the point that odd bits of my own experience were of unpredictable though indispensable importance in the effort to reconstruct the dynamics of his development. A spontaneous image of a large doll was the central structure by which I began to grasp his state of mind. Through a memory of a paper I had read, I was able to make a connection to the meaning of buffoonery. The association to my own dream of a spinning disk opened out into the full range of phenomena in the Oedipus complex, and the early formation of personality. The apparent ease with which my own associations led me to insights about the patient, which in turn facilitated further unfolding, was actually the result of hard work, especially a sustained attempt to understand and interpret his effort to depreciate me. So the hour I described was a culmination. The flow of ideas told me that my patient, somewhat relieved of his defenses, was in a position to hear difficult truths. His defenses now permitted him to face the previously unfaceable.

Although I was old enough to be his father, I felt, in this experience of approximation, a certain contemporary solidarity. We had worked out, through many prior hours, a means of communication that enabled me to phrase and him to hear the heart of the insights that arose from his associations and my own parallel stream of thinking. Such moments as these often do come toward the end of a period of treatment.

The patient's architectural work had improved in that time. He gave up the pattern of confusing his clients by a mixture of exciting but impractical proposals. He recognized a fear of submission to their needs and was able to take pride in his very valuable imagination. In addition, he began to speak at length about his relationship to his wife, as if notic-ing problems in that area which he had previously sought to exclude from discussion. Clearly, as the end approached, I no longer posed a threat to him as an authority figure. By then, however, it seemed best not to suggest a continuation of his treatment for the time being, and we parted. I thought I might someday see him again. I was willing to limit any impulse to acquaint myself with more than he wanted me to. I was willing, that is, to let him remain a stranger in the ways he still wished to be one.

Anyone intending to become a psychotherapist or psy-choanalyst must learn how to treat strangeness with respect. He listens carefully to the remarks that the person sitting in the chair or lying on the couch is making, and at the same time pays attention to his own stream of associations to those remarks. A division in the therapist's listening mode into an immediately responding aspect and another, which observes and meditates upon those responses, makes possible a free-dom of intuition and also the careful evaluation of what is intuited. Attentive listening is a skill that keeps on develop-ing over the entire course of training and practice, and is one of the principal subjects of this book. It depends on being comfortable with that stranger within, the unconscious, and on being able to recognize meaning in one's own spontane-ous thoughts as well as the patient's. When a patient begins to recognize that careful observation and logical thinking can lead toward a grasp of the complexities, that it's possible to identify threads of continuity as they develop and weave a pattern, then a feeling of hope develops, and he begins to express himself more freely.

Yet it is not only an accumulation of insights that open the eyes of the patient to his own unconscious, and release in him a freedom to function which he had never known. The patient will not have learned all he needs to know in his therapy, no matter how well it goes. He will have to continue the process of trying to understand himself as he faces the inevitable impasses that are part of anyone's life. He acquires, through long periods of observing the therapist's thought process, directly and indirectly, a sense of the therapist's capacity to make connections among disparate observations, and to assign meanings, tentatively and hypothetically at first, more surely later, or to discard what seems to be erroneous. This is not to say that he becomes the therapist's double or takes over his mentality wholesale. Such mimicry, seen particularly among the patients of charismatic analysts, indicates a failed treatment, the swamping of individuality by desperate fusion with the therapist's characteristic way of being and behaving.

What the patient acquires for himself under good conditions is a way of thinking, an awareness of the importance of the unconscious, a capacity to free associate and to notice connections that would have escaped him before his treatment. In addition to the expected results of successful treatment—the amelioration or disappearance of symptoms, an overall growth of understanding of himself and others, and greater emotional stability—these improvements in his capacity to think equip the patient to deal with new problems as they arise. These by-products of the struggle to overcome emotional suffering through understanding its unconscious roots are the special gain of psychoanalytic therapy. Symptom-oriented therapies, be they based on drugs, hypnosis, behavior modification, or certain kinds of group experiences, in ignoring underlying meanings do not teach such lessons.

The prospective psychotherapist or psychoanalyst who learns to respect strangeness will be wary of regarding patients as duplicates of others or as examples of a category of pathology. Should he succumb to such a temptation, the constructive tension that accompanies an encounter with the strange, which leads to experiences of discovery for both therapist and patient, is lost. Unable to sustain a sense of the patient as a unique human being, the therapist is pushed by anxiety toward intellectualizing about the patient's life as a collection of parts. It is true that he must find a way to think about the various aspects of the patient's life in order to give them the detailed attention needed for understanding. But if he's out of touch with the total life before him, his judg-ments are unbalanced, and the patient tends to lose heart, as someone worked on rather than related to. The therapist whose view comprehends the whole *and* the parts continu-ally discovers, defines, and corrects. His view is neither static nor out of control. It is steady and evolving.

This book describes the problems and opportunities en-countered by a prospective therapist as he develops. It traces his progression from the first stirrings of an interest that is defined in time as appropriate to the vocation of therapist, through college, medical school, residency train-ing in psychiatry, and studies in psychoanalysis. The second part of the book deals with the actual practice of psychother-apy and psychoanalysis and attempts to provide answers to the difficult question: How is the work actually done?

Throughout his career, the therapist is subjected to con-tradictory influences which may at best provide useful bal-ance or at worst tear him apart. Reason entices him toward its cool satisfactions, while the pleasures of the imagination beckon. The attempt to objectify his patients tends to de-prive them of recognizable wholeness, but the therapist gets nowhere if all he does is to have an ordinary relationship to another human being. He has to study each patient in a way that gives him a grasp of conflict. Knowing a great deal about the brain does not qualify a person as an expert on the mind. Throughout his career the therapist stands between the ob-jectivity of science and the inwardness of poetry. In con-fronting the resulting tensions, he fashions himself.

Subjectivity being such an important part of the work, it

seems best to speak directly of my own life. Since, no matter how well analyzed or well trained, a therapist can never function except as a person, within the context of his own emotional life, understanding of this complex work should begin with the therapist himself.

2.

CHILDHOOD
BEGINNINGS

The personal discovery of psychotherapy as feasible work—
that moment when one is first aware that this is a field that
fits one's talents and aspirations—is preceded by many
phases that prepare the ground.

A colleague, born in Greece, whose father died before he
could remember, grew up with a stepfather who was
French. The discovery that this man, whom he loved, was
not his biological father took place at the advent of World
War II. He was six at the time. The family had to uproot itself
and seek refuge wherever possible. There were many stops
along the way, but eventually they were able to settle in
London. This upheaval paralleled the process of rethinking
that was forced upon him by the new knowledge of his
parentage. The success of his family's new life, and his own
capacity to find his way to a satisfactory relationship with his
stepfather, fostered a sense of optimism about how crises
may turn out. Also, his initial stunned awareness of the different identity of the man he considered his father formed the
core of an ongoing concern with the nature of relationships,
familial resemblances, and personal devotion. Genealogical
questions preoccupied him in adolescence as he attempted
to attain a firm grasp of his origins. His interest gradually
enlarged to include the origins of others, as explored in physical anthropology. In his twenties, he became concerned

with the beginnings of emotional development as well, and turned to the study of clinical psychology, and particularly child development. His imaginative capacities permitted him to organize vast amounts of information about his patients into coherent wholes. His flexibility, born of good experiences with crisis, had a cognitive dimension. He could invent and consider a wide range of explanations for whatever phenomena he studied.

Another colleague was the only child of taciturn, religious parents. A lonely childhood was relieved by contact with his athletic, sociable uncle, with whom he spent Saturday afternoons at football games. The emotional paralysis of his parents introduced a similar element in his own development, a tendency to conform too easily, a certain shyness, a limited range of expression. But his innate intelligence, in league with the influence of his lively uncle, gave him a view of his parents and himself from the outside.

An urge to help his hypochondriacal mother expanded into interests that led him to medical school, and the deeper, ongoing preoccupation with understanding how his parents affected his development spurred him to study psychiatry. He had the advantage of an acute and ready wit, which stood against the dourness of his parents, yet there remained a tendency to subside into the low-level depression that was there almost from the start of his life.

I can see from my own life how the stages unfold, with landmarks visible at expected times. The appendectomy when I was six posed a challenge to my capacity to meet trauma with a countering organization, which turned out to be a defense called "identification with the aggressor." By thinking of myself as just like the surgeon who operated on me, I magically acquired his power and gained relief from helplessness.

In addition to the Oedipal crisis, with the surgeon in the role of castrator/father, there was the influence of my mother. Circumstances had set a special stage for my birth.

A brother died of complications following appendicitis during my mother's pregnancy with me. I was, simply by my birth, a reparative presence, and much of what followed was a simple unfolding of this fact. In being a reminder of someone else, I was even the object of a kind of transference. My mother had become deeply depressed because of her loss, and also because she had found herself with Parkinson's disease in her twenties. The tremor in her left hand became, for me, a symbol of her state. I confused her emotional and neurological conditions, unable for a long time to realize that in certain respects they were quite separate matters. Children make connections like that, and then base their inner lives on them.

I did my best to provide reassurance to her by doing what she asked. I suppose the possibility of my own early death made the appendectomy experience even more frightening for us. She had an enthusiastic and joyful side, which appeared especially when she played the piano, and with this activity the tremor disappeared. There were memorable moments when, at large family gatherings, we all sang for hours while she played. These experiences kept alive the notion that a disability could, under the right circumstances, be transcended, a most important piece of knowledge for a therapist when he is being flooded with feelings of helplessness and hopelessness. The fact that relief can come in a moment dispels the limitless aspect of these feelings but, unfortunately, is easily forgotten. The analyst's cogent grasp of a patient's efforts to communicate may provide just that temporary relief which suggests how much more might await a more comprehensive sort of understanding. Or it may be in the form of an inadvertent sigh, or a chuckle, or an unwavering concentration, some sign of recognition that ministers instantly to the loneliness of emotional illness.

My mother's zest for learning sped me toward the education required for me to be of help to other people. My joy in the colors of maps, which represented unknown but real places, derived from her enthusiastic stories of faraway peoples. Her memorized poems and quotations from Shakespeare became a store of memory for me as well, which, appreciated in the beginning only as feats of the mind, were recognizably wise and beautiful later on. This was all part of the wonder and fascination of learning and knowing.

Another of the important contributions to my eventual choice of the work of the psychoanalyst came during the time that we lived on a street near Boston State Hospital. Going to school each day, my schoolmates and I passed the wrought-iron fence, and as often as not observed a crew of inmates weeding or raking nearby. Some, leaning their hands high against the iron bars, would beckon to us. Chilled with fear, we hurried to the safety of Miss Leary's fourth-grade classroom.

At night, from the distant and heavily screened porches, random screams and wails pierced the silence, as if to suggest suffering without rhyme or reason. And on our very street, a middle-aged man appeared each twilight, smoking his pipe while he shined the rocks that lined his driveway. My mother said not to call him "Benny the Boom Boom," as all my friends did. "He's sick," she said, her hand trembling. I didn't know what she could mean by "sick," but I know I felt respect for her judgment and her kindness. She was showing proper concern for an injured soul.

Children are exposed to unusual sights as a matter of course. I remember a man with a withered arm, said by my parents to be a bookie. I had the puzzle to solve of what a bookie was, in addition to figuring out how the withered arm was related to it. One thought about such matters involuntarily, out of fascination and fear and the urge to decipher the nature of the world. There was a classmate who had lost one joint of a finger. I thought she should be wearing some sort of bandage on the end, but it was healed, and strangely naked to one's gaze. I stole glances at her finger and could not approach her unselfconsciously. A child whose mother had died aroused in most of us an inexpressible fear, for his life was proof that the unthinkable was actually possible. He suffered from our inability to take him for granted like any other kid.

My mother's compassionate view of a disturbed man was an example to which I repeatedly returned. It helped me to avoid the temptation of dealing with fear through mockery and to keep hold of the sense of bewilderment long enough to get to the beginnings of comprehension. The strangeness of my dead brother's face in the photograph on a table in our home—the cause of so many of my mother's tears—the mystery of my own origins, of everyone's, were joined to the strangeness of a pipe-smoking man at dusk.

Three examples of the early lives of people who became therapists hardly exhaust the possibilities. Each therapist will have developed out of conflict, intent upon making sense of it to the extent of transforming that interest into a career which permits the tandem examination of the lives of others and one's own life. That career permits him to meditate on the boundaries that separate his life from the lives of his patients, and on the ways in which the past colors and shapes the present. What he has to offer originates as a by-product of the need to assuage his own pain, and to reach for a fuller life through the use of reason. It outgrows this origin over the course of training, establishing itself as reliably professional and not easily undone, though somewhere inside there remains the thread that winds its way back to childhood.

3.

DEVELOPMENTS
IN COLLEGE

The experience of being taught by accomplished teachers in any field fosters the desire to be accomplished as well. Such teachers serve as models for one's own aspirations to maturity and achievement. It helps even more to encounter someone who inspires one along specific lines of mastery. A course in my second year of college given by Dr. Henry Murray, a physician-psychologist who was also trained in biochemical research, suggested to me a possible future for myself. Murray is most widely known for his work on so-called projective tests, which make it possible for subjects to express what is within, in response to some stimulus presented to them. He is the co-inventor of the Thematic Apperception Test, a series of pictures of ambiguous interactions among people, about which the subject is asked to tell stories.

I was impressed with the care Murray gave to his lectures, which showed respect for his listeners, and by a contagious enthusiasm for his subject and for living, which came across in a jaunty style of dress and a ready smile. My own father's capacity for enthusiasm, a source of great encouragement to me over the years, played its unconscious role in my response to Murray. I found a particularly comfortable spot in the library, where my mood was peaceful and concentrated, a haven of communion between myself and the person who was a model to me, and systematically read all of his published work.

Toward the end of the course, Dr. Murray suggested that I think about a career in psychology. I was surprised and flattered, of course, and grateful. Like him, I wanted to combine the role of physician with the study of the mind.

Identification with such accomplished figures, free of the emotional complications of home life, facilitates growth. At college age, one's expanded awareness of the many ways life can be led stimulates the expectation that one will be able to find just the right pattern for oneself. For example, a colleague's relationship to a priest–social worker in the Peace Corps, a man who had dedicated himself to helping poor people in the Far East, became the means by which he was able to throw off the emotional ravages of a psychotic father. He decided to study medicine, and later specialized in psychiatry and psychoanalysis. His career focused on the application of psychoanalytic ideas to social issues, and he writes about the psychology of poverty.

Another colleague, from a close-knit family that had restricted his horizons, became friendly in the first confusing days of college with a young student from Mexico whose parents were concentration camp survivors. This friend was beset with concerns about his parents and confused about what to do with his life. But throughout his college career he continued to find many subjects that deeply interested him, and in moving from one to another, he pieced together a sense of himself. The friendship put my colleague in touch with his own confusion and encouraged him to find his way toward inner knowledge and satisfaction as well. Courses in literature developed his sense of the imagination as an organizer, a means by which different pieces of experience could be welded together into organic wholes. First he thought that he would write novels, then that he would study human development, then that he would make people well by being a physician, then that he would reach toward understanding the emotional life by being a psychoanalyst. It was the fresh experience of exploration and integration with his friend that had led him along this path.

In addition to my good fortune in having Henry Murray as a teacher, I took a course called Theories of Personality, which included a number of readings from Freud. We studied *The Psychopathology of Everyday Life,* which is about slips of the tongue and pen, events that, carefully understood, reveal the existence of an unconscious mind. *A General Introduction to Psychoanalysis* was made up of lectures on Freud's various discoveries. His descriptions of free association meant a great deal to me because I had long been fascinated by my own associations on the way to sleep, when I would enjoy tracing back a line of thinking through the odd details that linked one thought or image with another. Freud's elucidation of this pathway into the darkness of unconscious life evoked in me an experience of awe, a primal event in the choice of a lifework. The interlocking of my own native introspective tendencies and Freud's great discovery made a sturdy beginning.

Volunteer work in a state hospital also played a substantial role in initiating my professional development. A friend of mine had been so moved by the plight of hospitalized psychotic children that he originated a program to befriend them, which came to include adults as well. Scores of college students put in an afternoon a week in these institutions. The "Case Aide" program, the one I entered, involved fourteen students, each of whom was assigned a patient who was safe enough to discharge if proper arrangements could be made. Under the supervision of a social worker, we met with our patients once a week, and then spent two hours as a group, discussing our experiences.

The wards seemed endless in the great brick buildings.

The grounds were spacious, but the heavy bunches of keys that every nurse bore, the echoing slam of steel doors that left us enclosed with the patients, the bizarre or dead expressions on their faces, the monotonous rocking in their chairs, enforced an atmosphere in which people were turned in on themselves, as in a prison.

In encountering patients in a mental hospital, I was trying to carry my interest in psychology beyond the classroom. Entering the mental hospital was also a personal test, because the insane had been frightening to me since childhood. The conditions under which they lived, in the era just preceding the introduction of psychotropic drugs (the early 1950s), were still reminiscent of the nineteenth century, with enormous buildings full of people who were provided with the rudiments of bed and board, medical attention, "peaceful" grounds, and officious, closed-minded nurses. These walled-off refuges, created both for the patients and for a society unable or unwilling to confront them, were mysterious places, and I remembered, on first entering, that the old name for psychiatrist was "alienist." I was acutely aware that the inmates were a segregated lot. Why, I wondered, would I decide not to avoid them, as most others did? I later thought that perhaps it was like an exotic journey sought as a tonic for one's unseen self, which would emerge against a novel background. Or that it was like going among the lepers.

In that sense, there was the fear of going crazy oneself. One tended to think that people deliberately isolated had some disease that others would catch if they got too close. I grew up at a time when infectious disease was associated with a certain foreboding. Quarantine signs which marked the homes of the afflicted, even for a disease as mundane as measles, created grim thoughts in passersby. And there was a frightening aspect to direct exposure to completely deranged people. So it was salutary, and eventually a confirmation, to get over my initial recoil in the face of alien beings who lived in an atmosphere that smelled of Lysol and urine.

With Mrs. Margaret Sorensen, an obese woman of sixty-two, hospitalized for the past twenty-two years after a profound depressive withdrawal, there was, at first, a sense of futility. With the enthusiasm of the young and untried, I had thought perhaps she would greet me with open arms, so it was my first lesson that the help I wanted to offer was not necessarily welcome. Mrs. Sorensen, a veteran of three courses of electroshock therapy, with her dead blue eyes and with straggly gray hair gathered by the hospital attendants into a simple bun, was one of those who stared into the distance across the lawns. I said her name and mentioned my own and reached for her hand, finding it to be cold and boneless flesh. Then I told her, in a prepared speech, in which there was hardly a trace of conviction, that I was there to help her leave the hospital. No spark of interest altered her expression. I felt that I was trying to change her life against her will, or perhaps against her understanding, if indeed I could provide anything at all in such a place. Whatever my expectation, it wasn't met, and what surged through me was an impulse to leave, to leave immediately, and not attempt to make a change in the unchangeable. There was nothing to go on, no shred of hope on which to pin a future. My fear had given way to hopelessness in about five minutes.

I told her I would be back the next week, and dragged myself to the meeting our group had planned. I had little to tell my associates, but was less discouraged when I realized few had anything substantive to say. The group leader, a young and easygoing social worker, understood our feelings of fear and hopelessness. His saying that they were common to novices supported us against the impending sense of being as helpless as the patients. He explained that the possibility of confusing ourselves with them sometimes made us differentiate ourselves so completely that we could feel nothing for their plight or their state of mind, and sometimes swamped us with the feeling that there was no way to help them, that what we were doing was a useless academic gesture, an attempt to dog-paddle across an ocean. The social worker's provision of a context by one who had been there, so to speak, dispelled our dismay and rekindled our enthusiasm. To provide a context for hopelessness is to make it possible to bear it.

This experience was my version of a next step beyond books and talk about psychotherapy. I was lucky to have the opportunity, but if a person is ready to respond to what he needs, he can usually find a path. It was important to me to see that I could encounter the world of the insane and not be crippled by anxiety.

There was one student who could not. A pale and withdrawn fellow from Colorado, he did not discuss his case with the group. He seemed a bit more confused than the rest of us. Two years later I encountered him walking along the banks of the Charles River. He told me that he had chosen to become a geologist and that the experience at Metropolitan State had turned him away from medical school. Prior to that he had been considering a career in psychiatry. He said that it took him months to recover from his brief period on the back wards. His dreams had begun to get the better of him. One night he awoke in a sweat from a vision of his patient threatening him with a knife. He felt he was beginning to come apart. "I just couldn't take it," he told me.

The friend who founded the volunteer program went on to medical school, but to the surprise of everyone, did not become a psychiatrist. He is a general practitioner in a small town, preferring the ordinary human contact of such a practice to the more complicated and anonymous struggles of the psychiatrist's consultation room. Or perhaps his sorrow for those poor children and others like them proved more of a burden of feeling than he wished to be reminded of.

One friend of mine who was interested in being a psychologist decided to telephone practitioners at their offices and ask if she could question them about their work. Their views on the education most likely to prepare her for the sort of work she had in mind (she had a special interest in delinquent children) were somewhat different from the prescribed courses in that direction. She was able to form a picture of the satisfactions and frustrations ahead of her. This connection with the world beyond the university and its programs oriented her thereafter.

With the perspective provided by later experience, I can see that it was helpful to encounter mental patients without the insulation that would be provided by the role of medical student or resident. I was able to approach the strange world of the mental hospital in a way which helped to guarantee that as my education advanced I would not easily have the illusion that one could take possession of these people with an armamentarium of diagnostic categories, theories, and drugs. You need protection against the masses of information you are bound to encounter later on about the nature of mental and emotional illness. It is beneficial to have a primary experience with which to imprint on your mind the plight of patients, which is beyond all talk, and to get a sense of proportion about the nature of any attempt to provide a means of improvement. You understand clearly what a small figure you are in the face of another life. Only against such a background can you gradually come to know how large you may loom.

4.

MEDICAL SCHOOL: I

For the practitioner who uses pharmacological or other physical methods in the treatment of the emotionally and mentally ill, a medical education is of course required. Whether four years of medical school and a year of internship are essential for one who practices psychotherapy or psychoanalysis exclusively is another question.

Premedical curricula begin the process of sorting people according to their reaction to the subject matter, for there are those who take to the likes of biology, chemistry, and physics, and those who find that they cannot think their way through such material. Future physicians become part of an extremely competitive race for high grades, which are required for admission to medical school. This mad rush can be quite unattractive to a scholar of the mind, who may prefer graduate school in psychology.

Psychotherapy, psychoanalysis, psychiatry, clinical psychology—all these fields are in flux. Traditionally, a person who wanted to be a psychoanalyst had to be a physician-psychiatrist trained in one of the institutes whose standards were set by the American Psychoanalytic Association, which was (and is) itself a branch of the International Psychoanalytical Association, founded by Freud. In recent years, however, a growing number of institutes, which are not approved by the American Psychoanalytic Association, have begun to train nonphysicians. A college student contemplating a career as a therapist may prefer the clinical psychology path through graduate school, followed by one of these institutes. He will probably become part of the struggle by which they hope to be regarded as the equal of the older and more established institutes.

I had been aimed toward medicine since early in life and took to the premedical subjects with enthusiasm, but studies in psychology, and, increasingly, comparative literature, drew my attention. I was greatly affected by a book of short stories by Franz Kafka. The impact of "Metamorphosis," "The Hunger Artist," "The Great Wall of China," and the others led me to ponder just what it was in these works that arrested my mind in midmotion. Kafka had said that books should be like axes which break up the frozen seas within us. A fluid awareness of the human world depended on an ability to be open to all hopes and disappointments, struggle and bewilderment. This was one of the attractions of doing analysis, insofar as I could glimpse it by reading Freud: to be given genuine access to the entire emotional spectrum of other people's lives, and to be able to help them get access to it themselves.

The study of literature was to prove very useful to my efforts to form interpretations that would adequately capture the conflicts of patients. The literary and the clinical became mutually stimulating frames of reference. What I read in both seemed potentially useful to my everyday concerns with patients, although I did not read for pragmatic ends. I could never tell when some odd bit of knowledge or imagination would prove to be a facilitating link in the effort to arrive at an understanding of a patient.

Medical school crashed into my life when I was twenty-one. It meant strength and power, a rigor comparable to the education of a West Point cadet, based on seriousness of responsibility for the lives of others. One needed to become rocklike, practically inanimate in one's capacity to withstand emotional pressures, in order to make the salient judgments that would save lives. How rare it was later on to have a therapy patient whose life one had saved. How delicious to the lapsed physician to hear the courageous young woman with a devastating muscle disease say: "I wouldn't have made it through those first couple of years without your help, and now I really do want to live." Yet one knows as well that as a therapist/analyst one does foster life over death in the sense of lived over unlived life; the capacity to function, to realize potential, to flourish, over being thwarted, withdrawn, limited. And that some of one's ability to do such work depends on those years as a medical student, on one's deep identity as a physician, on a commitment to life over death. No matter how much of a heuristic subject psychoanalysis may be, it is above all a means to treat a suffering patient.

The spirit of medical school was to study—day and night. What there was to know covered the normal and the pathological throughout the entire span of life. The subjects had nothing to do with one's inner life, and in attending to them with such concentration we tended to get hardened. Whenever you give yourself over entirely to the external, you become, in a sense, annihilated. It was in the new friendships, the relationships to teachers (where such relationships were possible—one of mine was as cadaverous as the cadaver he taught us from, until he cracked a smile one day and illuminated the room), and most of all, in the relationships to patients that one found the saving humanity by which to soften the relentlessly dehumanizing effect of the study of medicine. We were willful young men and women. Our capability was less a matter of intelligence than of an unremitting effort of the will. We were pitting ourselves against the resistant information, the daily menu made up of the location and function of practically unpronounceable muscles, the staining propensities of all sorts of cells, that congeries of biochemical transformations known as the Krebs cycle, the complexly packed and mysterious brain. We would prevail over it all. Patients' lives depended on our doing so.

The information wasn't going to make itself known to us if only we let it flow in. The cultivation of the will would turn us into worthy objects of confidence, larger-than-life sources of hope for our future patients. Most of us were in our early twenties, mindless of the limits of our own years, though we dealt with death at every turn. The stance of the physician as one who is in possession of the secrets of life enabled us to deflect uncertainty, that emotion which would one day prove so valuable to those of us who became therapists.

I am describing the effect of medical education this way so as to define a contrast between its influence and that of the psychiatric and psychoanalytic education to come. This is not to say simply that it is a detour on the path toward sensitivity. It is that. Freud thought physicians had much to forget if they were to become good analysts. But it is also a training in detachment, which has a place. A therapist can't be of much use if he is flooded by empathy or overcome by his patient's hostility. He has to be able to think in order to supply what the patient can't think up on his own.

By educating the prospective therapist in the nature of the physical structures and processes that underly all human activity, medical school also contributes to a sense of the wholeness of the person. It helps to know a good deal about the brain and heart as organs, as well as about the mind and emotions as they manifest themselves consciously and unconsciously. The balance of one's judgment is enhanced by considerations of physical reality. I've mentioned the constructive tension generated by relating to the patient as a whole person, while studying the various ways in which he functions. I've also spoken of the importance of the associations of both the patient and oneself. The duality of mind/body generates another such polar tension, though with built-in safeguards against overestimating the force of the one or the other. The physician can easily remember that a patient may be suffering from physical disease as well as emotional problems. His headache may be a migraine or a symptom of a tumor, not only the result of an acute conflict with his employer. A patient's arthritic spine may be responsible for the pains in her hand. The wish to shoot her lover may be incidental.

And the sense of responsibility for preserving life, even if made subsidiary to the attempt to assess the meaning of a patient's statements, provides an overarching "holding environment"—to use D. W. Winnicott's term—within which a piece of therapy or analysis may unfold. This environment will itself have to be analyzed, to permit a patient to separate from his helping person in the end, and to face his responsibility for his own life, but in the meantime it will have facilitated the process that leads to that point. This is particularly true of disturbed patients whose fragmented sense of themselves may require the strong arms of one who is used to taking responsibility. In Chapter 12, I discuss my attempt to find forms of understanding that would enable me to encompass a vast range of confusing statements from a psychotic woman. A capacity to pit myself against the protracted mental onslaught of her deranged state came in good measure from medical school experiences of persisting where the pressures push one toward giving up. The example of many teachers paves the way. I can never forget an experience in the operating room in which the perspiring surgeon spent two hours searching the abdominal cavity for a small bleeding vessel that would have led to the patient's death if it could not have been found and ligated.

None of these advantages of a medical education is exclusively the property of the physician. But five years of medical school and internship do inculcate a set of attitudes that, properly modified in the years to follow, gives depth and balance to the work of the therapist and analyst.

5.

MEDICAL SCHOOL: II

The student of medicine is pulled between mastering voluminous detail and responding to the human beings he treats. The special problem for the future therapist is to stay in touch with feeling without losing the objectivity required for diagnosing and treating physical conditions. Sometimes, the proportions of tragedy to which he is a witness are so great that he cannot sustain continuing responsiveness. Wanting to cry out against the indifference of fate, he grows hard instead.

I was expected to follow Mrs. Geraldine Washington, a twenty-three-year-old woman, until her baby was two months old. This was the first trimester of her first pregnancy. I examined her monthly, along with the obstetrics resident, and, after each examination, discussed with her whatever problems she was having.

Mrs. Washington asked me to call her Gerry, and I did not correct her use of "Doctor" in almost every sentence. She was making me into a doctor by reminding me that I was supposed to be one.

In the ninth month, Gerry's appointments took place every week. Just before her due date, a trickle of amniotic fluid appeared and she was examined in the obstetrical clinic every day. The resident repeatedly sent her home and told her to call if a gush of fluid occurred. When, after several days, signs of infection appeared, a consultant was called in. At this time, her abdomen had become extremely tender. She had a high fever. This quiet, cooperative woman had become rapidly weakened and delirious.

It was apparent that the amniotic sac was now infected. Frantic attempts to elicit signs of continuing life in the baby were of no avail. The treatment for this condition was the removal of the uterus and its contents en bloc.

I was in the recovery room after the surgery. Bewildered as she had been, and highly medicated, it would be a few hours before Gerry would regain her senses and begin to understand the loss she had suffered.

I became less and less emotional, without being aware of it. I had somehow anesthetized myself against her grief. I checked her pulse, counted her respirations, and noted the rate at which the yellow drops were entering her circulation from the bottle hanging above the bed. I was an observing scientist. I left her side for a while to discuss her condition with the nursing staff. When I returned, her eyes were opening slowly. "You must be knocked out," I said, rather mechanically. "Gerry," I said, "Gerry, I'm sorry to tell you this. You had to have a hysterectomy."

"What about my baby?" she said hesitantly.

I told her that it couldn't be saved. Her face was contorted with pain and I had to look away. I was ashamed that I was one of those who had failed her. This wasn't the profession I had anticipated with such enthusiasm. It taught lessons I didn't want to learn, about human error with tragic results and a sense of limits.

But learning from death was to be an everyday matter. Autopsies gave us retrospective knowledge by which we might do better the next time. And grief could be the beginning of something new and good. Few people fail to learn such lessons in life, but the medical student learns them at an earlier age and in more frequent and insistent ways. Yet for me there was nothing useful or good in the case of Gerry Washington, only the baleful warning that a single failure of judgment may lead to death. I was not stimulated by this lesson, so much as the involuntary bearer of it.

You aren't aware in medical school of deciding to remain sensitive or to let yourself become hardened. The pressure of the training runs you ragged and your energies are devoted to remaining effective. Discussions with classmates are helpful, if you can find a way to express your pain. Often, however, you cannot say how you feel because you don't know, or are afraid the feelings you recognize will undermine the effort to become strong or will be regarded by others as evidence of a lack of aptitude for the work.

Sometimes an electric excitement obscures the human tragedy. One of my gynecology professors, with a worldwide reputation for his daring approach to cancer, radiated such a degree of confidence, and such pleasure in doing his surgical work well, that one could forget that when he finished, the patient was left with half a pelvis.

Some medical students find themselves responding with anger to the apparent coldness of residents, faculty, and their own peers, all of whom may not be as cold as they appear to be. I often asked embarrassing questions of those residents who didn't seem to give a thought to the person in the bed or on the table. One may be regarded as unprofessional if one focuses on questions of the emotions. The state of mind required to consider them is different from the usual one of physicians, perhaps especially young, up-and-coming physicians, and it tends to cut off the flow of medical dialogue. Such discussions do not appear to have a natural place, except sometimes as an afterthought, perhaps in response to guilt.

By the latter half of medical school, there is a good deal of attention to presenting case material to distinguished attending physicians, which is to say crisply, efficiently, factually. They represent the highest authority in clinical matters. You are learning from them how to behave, to present faceless expressions to patients, to ask questions rapidly to cover the necessary ground, and to give recommendations with a tone that elicits compliance with a minimum of protest. You are learning how to take over another person's body. Usually you don't think much about the regressive forces you are setting in motion, with the frightened patient feeling more and more like a child, hoping for competence in the persons who hold his life in their hands, but without a means to measure competence. The regression may even seem desirable to the physician, by its reducing of questions to a minimum.

In time, the medical student develops the will to face all situations as they come along. As you assume more and more responsibility and go on to an internship, you do not hesitate to ring the distant phone in the middle of the night, to announce death, to rise from the callroom bed at any hour, to insert a needle to get a blood sample, or to hold the baby down so that your otoscope may help determine if there is, in fact, an ear infection. You feel yourself growing stronger and stronger, your will reinforced and invigorated by the many successful treatments that modern medicine affords.

But your blunted sensitivity cannot be turned on and off like a faucet. How can you be both strong and sensitive, when your strength seems to derive, in part, from insensitivity? To feel fully again is, for most of us, an achievement of a later phase, when confidence and a less hectic schedule provide the room in which to find our human self again. Discipline applied to the emotions, for the sake of carrying out painful but indispensable services on behalf of patients, can be a precious legacy, assuming that the discipline has not become so depersonalizing that it results in the graduation of a robot dressed in a pinstriped suit and carrying a black bag.

6.

FROM MEDICAL SCHOOL
TO PSYCHIATRIC
RESIDENCY

My interest in psychiatry grew slowly during medical school. A required course or two was sandwiched in among everything else, but toward the end the pace slowed, and I was able to arrange an elective month. Besides the routine case conferences, in which experienced clinicians showed how information about a patient could be organized into understanding, I encountered two other interesting areas of endeavor: the budding attempts of a young professor to develop an effective brief therapy for crisis situations; and the psychological and social effects of urban renewal.

The crisis work was exciting. I knew next to nothing about therapy, but was scheduled for patients much like a child being placed on a two-wheeled bicycle for the first time. I had to make sense of what I was hearing, and quickly. The professor supervised me closely, the parent's steadying hand. I was delighted to find that I had a modicum of success. The case I remember best was that of a twenty-two-year-old woman whose husband had abandoned her with a three-month-old child. She had straggly blondish hair which fell across her face, and the tears ran down her pale and freckled cheeks. She was near panic and had no relatives in Boston. Her husband's parents were ashamed of their son's behavior and offered help, but the patient did not want them in her tiny apartment. Their relations had not been pleasant and she blamed them for fomenting discord between herself and her husband. She had nowhere to turn. After listening to her anguished story of being herself abandoned by her father when she was seven, I enlisted the aid of a social worker to help with practical details of child care, and then tried to show her the connection between her response then and now, without trying to play down the very real loss of her husband. She had an acquaintance who lived a few blocks from her home, and she now managed to ask for her companionship, which helped greatly. After six sessions, she was much calmer and on her way to making a reasonable plan to cope. It was good to feel that a helpful attitude could make a difference.

I also became a member of a group of diversely trained professionals that was studying the effects of demolishing a long-established neighborhood. The people were being forced to find new places to live. This brought into play many subjects, including social anthropology, which had interested me in college. Studies of Irish and Jewish culture, of neighborhood structure, of patterns of immigration (Oscar Handlin's *The Uprooted* proved especially illuminating), were vivified in being applied to this problem. Studies of grief which had been carried out in the same hospital after the disastrous Coconut Grove nightclub fire some fifteen years earlier proved to be relevant to helping people who were losing so much of what they had taken for granted all their lives. The combining of disciplines reinforced my sense of the unity of all knowledge and demonstrated that any piece of information might eventually yield insight. Knowing a family's immigration history, for example, gave one a set of beginning facts from which to imagine what life might have been like for them. This, in turn, would bear heavily upon how the necessity to leave the old neighborhood would affect them.

I had become accustomed to looking for supplements to the regular training. Among these were the mental hospital volunteer program, a month at a medical school in England, and, later on, several months at Anna Freud's Hampstead Clinic in London. Such opportunities must be sought out. A year abroad between college and medical school can be a great benefit to one's growth. The subject of study needn't be directly related to one's career as a psychiatrist or psychoanalyst. You can't tell what will prove applicable. What matters is the pleasure you get in widening your horizons and being enriched as a human being. Living elsewhere stimulates new perspectives and a more independent sense of yourself. The best medical programs, even those that try the most to facilitate the growth of students, are insufficient for any individual who wants to find his own path.

In the transitional year of internship, I worked in a large municipal hospital. I began to see all my patients with a psychiatric eye, no matter what the physical illness. In a two-month rotation on the psychiatric ward, the main task was to sort out entering patients for disposition. All the casualties of the night were brought to the locked ward for safekeeping. I made daily rounds with the resident, who spent ten minutes or so with each new admission. Some, he thought, could go home with relatives, some should be kept in the hospital for treatment of physical problems such as delirium tremens, some could go to state hospitals for a period of treatment, some to the court for disposition. Life-changing decisions were made in ten minutes! I took for granted a physician's social power and hardly questioned the procedures. This was what had to be done, I told myself, learning from the cool composure of the resident. Inevitably, you behave like your first models. You try to fit into the field as you find it, for better or worse. Only later, when you finally have your wits about you, can you make personal judgments about the value and appropriateness of many actions that, in the beginning, you simply took for granted.

The question of what kind of internship best prepares you for psychiatric training is not easily answerable. The idea of a rotating internship, with experience in several specialties, rounding out one's medical training proper, is appealing, but if you have a strong interest in internal medicine, surgery, pediatrics, or some other specialty, staying with it may be more advantageous to the psychiatrist's background. Perhaps pediatrics is the most obviously relevant, for the therapist or analyst will always be concerned with infancy and childhood, whether or not he actually treats children. In so many ways it is the child in the patient who has to be brought to light and understood. But anyone who doesn't want to spend a year dealing with the physical problems of children should certainly not do so. Responding to your inner promptings should, at this point and hereafter, be the primary consideration. An interest in the mind will naturally prompt you to be a careful observer, and the stress of physical illness on patients will reveal how they function. So will the stress of being the physician, or assisting him or her.

During my internship it became necessary to investigate residency training programs, and I became acutely aware that the psychiatrist's concerns were so radically different, the pattern of his activity so removed from that of other practitioners of medicine, that they might have been pursuing two different professions. I asked myself whether I wanted to turn away from the medicine I had come to know and love. I had found the study of diagnosis and treatment so deeply satisfying and often so productive of immediate results that I was reluctant to set it aside. On the other hand, psychiatry drew me toward the myriad problems of human existence. It embraced the totality of my education and all curiosity about how people are constituted. This proved compelling enough to compensate me for what I had to leave behind. In coming to terms with the fundamental fact that my efforts would have to be exerted in a specific direction, with affirmation and renunciation two sides of the same coin, I felt strong.

I decided to study psychiatry in a large university medical center, instead of a state hospital or small psychoanalytically dominated program, because I didn't want to segregate myself any more than necessary.

That was twenty-five years ago. Today residencies are uniformly oriented toward the organic. A typical psychiatric resident does not move far from mainstream medicine, but even so there are choices to be made among programs. The main consideration from the point of view of the future therapist or analyst should be the widest possible exposure to psychiatric patients and psychiatric thought. I would not limit my choices to the few centers where analysts are influential, unless those centers offer a comprehensive view of all other modes of psychiatric thought, in which case one has the best of both. I was quite satisfied with the residency I chose, with its camaraderie, its guidance, and its development of my interest in dynamic psychotherapy and psychoanalysis, but today, with the burgeoning of information about organic factors in mental illness, you owe it to yourself and to your patients to know all the rest too, and to subject yourself to the conflicts that are associated with choosing among alternatives. An analytic orientation will not benefit from the sidestepping of issues related to drug treatment or any other therapeutic modality. Every experience can contribute depth to your reflections, particularly if you are forced to ask yourself exactly what you believe and believe in.

The residency program I chose was only a few years old. There were few enough social workers, psychologists, occupational therapists, administrative personnel, so that we knew one another well. I think of the weather as sunny when I started, fine, clear weather—a reflection, I believe, of the enthusiasm with which I came into the conference room at 8 A.M. every day, ready for work, for strenuous discussion, for good fellowship and knowledge. Throughout, the educational process occurred in groups, notwithstanding the privacy of individual therapy and supervision. Psychotherapy occupied the center of attention, psychotherapy with people of all ages.

Soon after I began my residency, John Kennedy was nominated for President. For the next few years, with the emergence of a new generation, there was a sense of hope. The mild apathy of the Eisenhower fifties disappeared into excited talk of the civil rights movement, the Peace Corps, and other forms of public service. A social revolution was soon to come, but we were still in the period before the advent of the contraceptive pill, the dangerous fun of LSD, the assassination of five political leaders, before the young thought that they could change the world, taking their effective opposition to the war in Vietnam as a model. We were products of the values of the Depression and World War II, and social order still had meaning.

The tenor of the times affects psychiatric residency training more than it does any other medical specialty. It isn't just a question of what moneys are available for research and teaching (that too); it is primarily what values are dominant in the society. Psychoanalysis had been energized during World War II by the application of its principles to the traumas of warfare. After the war, their use in the treatment of more lingering psychological casualties made a strong impression on the consciousness of the public as well as the medical profession. There was a great demand for training. By 1960, most departments of psychiatry were headed by psychoanalysts. There was a broad range of other interests represented as well: The tranquilizers and the first antidepressants were calling attention to the still young field of neurophysiology. Electroshock therapy and other physical methods of treatment were respectable. There was a lively interest in how ward milieu affected patients. At the heart of it was the principle that the early experiences of patients set the stage for what would happen later, and we could therefore help by showing them the connections. If they could get a grip on their own histories, they could change.

The white uniform of psychiatric residents went out in the middle 1960s. It became unseemly to differentiate status in an obvious way, and an egalitarian wind of freedom wafted through the stale halls of mental hospitals. This change in the uniform singled out psychiatry alone among medical specialties for a leveling of status, a trend of which one contemporary manifestation is the demand by psychologists for hospital privileges without having to be supervised by a medically trained person, and another, the claims of a variety of lay groups to an expertise in psychotherapy equal to that of psychiatrists. Psychiatry's reaction is evident today in the primarily biological orientation of training programs. Psychiatrists have returned to the medical mainstream, leaving psychotherapy largely behind. Physicians who practice it, and lay groups that claim special knowledge of it, often contend for the same patients.

In the sixties, it became disrespectful, uneconomical, and actually unconstitutional to keep patients locked up indefinitely, and the mental hospitals began to empty out. The planners thought that an array of effective drugs administered in community mental health centers would stabilize ex-patients, who could then be reintegrated into society. This has not always proved to be the case. By 1984, one third of the homeless were former mental patients, and a man who was unable to get an appointment in a mental health clinic shot twenty people to death in a McDonald's restaurant. There is growing agreement that psychosis and depression are organically caused and best treated pharmacologically. Financial pressures for the more affordable—that is, the shortest-term—therapies and for the use of drugs are determining much that happens in the field of psychiatry. Attention to the unconscious and the dream has been deleted from many kinds of treatment that are called therapy. Familiar forms of research, so much less problematic than the study of subjective life, are crowding out the old concerns among people who are medically trained.

Along with the remedicalization of psychiatry has come a tendency to reclassify psychoanalysis as one of the humanities, which has the effect of reading it out of the halls of medicine. A number of psychoanalytic theoreticians are in the vanguard of redefining psychoanalysis as a branch of hermeneutics, which is the effort to reconstruct the meaning of ambiguous texts. The physics of his age served Freud as a model for his theories, and he considered psychoanalysis to be a natural science, characterized by a search for causes— as expressed, for example, by the apparent discovery that hysterical patients had all been seduced as children. But with his renunciation of this theory, he entered upon an extended study of the role of fantasy life in the formation of symptoms, and much analytic work is devoted to clarifying the difference between how events were experienced and their more likely objective nature. The belief that one was seduced does not automatically mean that it happened as remembered, or at all, or, on the other hand, that it did not happen as remembered. One contemporary school holds that all experience is fictive and unobjectifiable. Its members say that what has been presented as the systematic pursuit of a method aimed toward uncovering the truth is, instead, a process by which attention is given to finding meanings, which may vary in the context of different analyst-patient combinations, each of which generates its own fictions. I am summarizing numerous individual views which differ among themselves. But all of them are far from the original scientific tenor that Freud brought to the field. Lines of thinking such as I've described have a tendency to reduce the validity of psychoanalysis in the eyes of the medical community, and to increase the risk of alienation for any psychiatrist with the temerity to study it.

At the same time, those who would drum psychoanalysis out of medicine are still a minority and may well prove to be mainly products of an age not notable for its introspection. As I began by noting, such swings of the Zeitgeist generally affect psychoanalysis. The fact is that residents consistently still ask for courses in psychoanalytic theory and practice, sensing perhaps that something vital is missing from a psychiatry that focuses only on the organic or on behaviorism—that is, on science as defined by the criteria of logical positivism, a school of philosophy that once dominated all science but that has itself become discredited with time.

7.

PSYCHIATRIC RESIDENCY:

FIRST YEAR

To deal with psychosis or neurosis is to deal with whole lives. This is not focal pathology in need of the correct drug. It's not a kidney stone waiting to pass, or, if worse comes to worst, to be removed surgically. It's a long-standing adjustment to living, gone awry. What the therapist has to approach it with is knowledge, intuition, patience, and language.

The psychiatric resident's lack of understanding of this new kind of care, which doesn't yield to traditional procedures, is hard to bear after five years of medical training. He has to come to terms with being a novice again and give up the insolence he has brought to the ward from medical school.

What he learns is his limits, at first with a disappointment that can become outright depression, later on with a touch of enthusiasm for the quality of reality in those limits, which are the only anchor point for an assessment of the possible. He cannot know how much he can do unless he can come to see what is beyond him, or, perhaps, beyond anyone, though the latter is always in question. It is also true that when he learns to do more, he begins to see the vastness of what he cannot do. The creation of a boundary between what can be changed and what cannot is the very locus of professional judgment.

My first patient was a twenty-eight-year-old man, who had been brought to the emergency room the night before by his landlady. She had broken into his apartment, to find him living in squalor. Masses of fungus had grown out of discarded food in the sink, and the patient smelled bad. Furthermore, he made no sense, grinning foolishly when she tried to find out whether he felt ill, and he resisted her when, with the aid of the janitor, she tried to take him to the hospital.

The next morning, I attempted to interview Martin Brinkman in his room on the ward. He appeared dazed and emaciated. There was little response to my questions, except transient eye contact when I told him that he looked frightened. This was like a match flare in pitch darkness, but I failed to include it in my initial note, in which I described the patient's behavior and appearance, and the normal results of a physical examination. I recommended that attempts be made to locate relatives, which the social worker was able to do. His family lived in a city two hundred miles away, and consisted only of his mother. She indicated that her son had decided to move five months earlier, after an unhappy relationship with a girl. Mr. Brinkman had previously been a loner and the relationship had been full of tribulation, with the girl teasing him mercilessly about his shyness and eccentricity. The patient's father had been in a mental hospital twice, and was now an alcoholic whose whereabouts were unknown.

I wrote down "Probably schizophrenic" at the end of my note, and the ward psychiatrist agreed. I undertook a period of extended evaluation, while studies were made to rule out things like a blood clot pressing on the brain or metabolic disease, which might produce a similar picture. Current diagnostic procedures for brain pathology are much more efficient and accurate than those current in 1960.

In psychodynamic terms, the schizophrenic's thought

process is believed to have been shattered by the release of uncontrolled aggression. Poorly developed defenses against the return of infantile rage have broken down, and the ability to think clearly has been impaired. Occasional flashes of logic give way to incoherence. Unprovoked bursts of emotion—be they anger, sentimental sadness, sexual attraction, or help-lessness—may be followed by stunned withdrawal, preoccupation with hallucinated voices, or delusional ideation of a paranoid type. The resident does well to simply subject him-self to this confusion and to experiment with his own inter-ventions, some of which will appear to have an effect. But his objectivity will inevitably flag under the pressure, and his mind wander. Remembering the events of an hour is easier when he learns to subdivide the sessions by subject or mood (his own or the patient's). Any structure in a period of interac-tion breaks it down into more manageable pieces.

When he compares his experiences with the impressions of other staff, he forms a fuller picture of the patient. Confer-ences that focus on the patient complement his ideas. His supervisor accompanies him into the intricacies of his experi-ence as a therapist, and the skillful veteran's views contrib-ute to the growth of perspective. Reading in the vast litera-ture of schizophrenia, that gulag of deranged mental forms, makes available another kind of support. The emphasis from all sources on the extreme difficulty of doing therapy with such patients tells the resident that he is in good company, that it is not his own deficiencies which make the work so difficult.

The enthusiasm of the beginner, armed with five years of medical training, often facilitates success. The first-year resident approaches the task with determination and the excitement of finally doing the work he has chosen for him-self. The schizophrenic's overall hopelessness, based in part on an inability to reconstitute himself, tends to invade the minds of people in contact with him, and the resident's hopefulness can counterbalance it, particularly if he is working with a patient having his or her first schizophrenic break. Two thirds of such patients tend to recover, so that he is likely to have a successful experience.

In the first hour, Mr. Brinkman shuffled into my office, flopped in the chair, and laid his head on my desk, his arms covering his face. I was irritated by this seeming lack of respect for me. "Why don't you sit up and tell me about yourself," I said.

The patient looked at a small Matisse print of a woman, grinned, and muttered something unintelligible. I said: "Do you know where you are?" Meeting silence, I explained: "You are in a mental hospital, because you are having a breakdown."

The patient grinned again, and muttered something I couldn't understand. He suddenly filled the silence with: "Shit, man, full of it." I thought he was right. I didn't know what I was doing. I tried to remain observant.

"You're angry with me," I said finally. I should have stopped at this point and watched for a response, but I added: "You're confused. We're going to be giving you some tests here and I'll be seeing you every day for a while. Perhaps we'll be giving you some medicine to make you feel better." I talked about what "we" would do rather than what "I" would do, drawing strength from the alliance with others.

"You have shut the cabinet, haven't you," said the patient, grinning again. His pale blue eyes focused directly on my own. He started to clear his throat over and over.

"Yes, for now," I said, as if having a normal conversation.

After the session, which lasted twenty minutes or so, I made some notes, which did not include fleeting impressions of contact or my sense of inadequacy when the patient told me that I was full of shit. Two days later, I sat in my office with my supervisor. As he listened carefully and then asked me to discuss my thoughts without notes, to talk especially about the way the patient made me feel, I remembered these observations. I was impressed with the amount of information stored inside my mind, which emerged only when I stopped trying to be so orderly. When I described how the patient laid his head on my desk, the supervisor saw a gesture of contact, "leaning on" an object that represented me. My irritation now appeared ridiculous.

With further interviews and supervisory sessions, I began to feel sorry for Mr. Brinkman. But then he would insult me or make some gesture that would renew my anger and resentment. He simply sensed my mood and reacted. He became known on the ward as a troublemaker. He turned over dishes during meals, spat at the window of the nurses' station, and tore up the psychologist's rating sheets during the psychological examination. Few people expressed any liking for the man, except for a student nurse whose job it was to get to know him a little, and accompany him to various places in the hospital.

A course of trifluoperazine, one of the more powerful tranquilizers, soon toned down his provocative behavior, an improvement that probably reflected more than a purely pharmacological effect. What begins with a drug soon affects the world of relationships. A calmer resident and staff were now working with a calmer patient.

Many patients become accessible to psychotherapy only when they are calmed by an appropriate psychotropic substance. But medication may alleviate the symptoms without affecting the basic pathology, and, in so doing, reduce the motivation of both patient and therapist to pursue psychotherapy in a serious way. This effect is frequently ignored today because drugs are so regularly employed and so powerful. It is particularly true in hospital environments.

In our interviews, the patient began to give a more complete picture of himself. He had had a miserable childhood in a small Nevada town. His father was an alcoholic ex-convict and his mother worked as a waitress. He came back to an empty house after school from the time he was five years old. Loneliness was never far away. He felt most comfortable with animals, particularly a cat he had had until he was fifteen. The girlfriend who left him was his very first. Anguished by the loss, he couldn't sleep, began to hallucinate, and then, in a panic, left home, in search of some release. In Los Angeles, he worked briefly as a taxi driver, and then began to drink cheap wine until he was intoxicated most of the time and unable to leave his room at all.

We talked mostly about the effect on his sanity of losing his girlfriend. I tried to link that loss to his background of neglect, wondering to myself about the possible genetic predisposition, in view of his father's breakdowns. The patient responded with a growing reality sense, and by forming relationships among ward staff and other patients, always remaining essentially private but becoming noticeably more of a participant. In occupational therapy, he painted a striking bird on a ceramic plate, something so vibrant and alive, and in such contrast to his demeanor, that we all saw great cause for hope.

He was discharged in five weeks, still on medication, with follow-up therapy planned for an indefinite period. However, the patient quickly became careless about his appointments, and called one day to say that he was moving back home and would not be coming anymore.

I had wanted to examine this patient's feelings at close range, in the protected context of my role, but was vaguely fearful of the seductions of psychotic thought. This is the typical conflict for the therapist of such an individual. The availability of drugs spared me such contact until he was less disturbed. Drugs modulate the intensity of psychotic behavior that the therapist must confront, and in achieving this, they make it possible for a motivated therapist to use his skills to greater effect. Only a few can tolerate the extremes of psychosis. Medication makes it possible for many more to treat such disturbed patients and for many more disturbed patients to be treated, unless the effects of medication are regarded as sufficient in themselves.

The main problem facing the beginning therapist is to achieve a personal state of restraint in which he may comfortably observe the patient, and himself as the observer. But the power of the physician is often too tempting to forgo. He writes orders, prescribes drugs, gives directions, and will sometimes threaten his patients, openly or subtly, using the reward of a weekend pass, say, to evoke "better behavior," or a locked room to punish "disruptions." Such lesson-teaching is a kind of conditioning. It is true that external controls in various forms are often required, especially in the beginning, to reassure certain patients that however out of control their minds may be, they have entered an environment in which others have the power to control them. A calming effect is often observed, with psychotherapy a possibility.

The characteristic tendency, however, is to replace therapy with drugs. Power is addicting. The physician must learn to free himself from its siren song, a necessarily gradual process. Only as he appreciates the deeper satisfactions and consequences of understanding a difficult person, without concern about losing self-esteem, will he be able to stop relying on medical power. He can then learn to become comfortable with the patient as a fellow human being instead of an object to be controlled, under whatever rationale of helping.

Psychotic patients, who account for most of the first-year resident's caseload, can almost always benefit from medication. However, the prescribing habit may then carry over into the treatment of many other diagnostic categories, the depressives above all, and deny the resident and the patient an opportunity to see what therapy in a chemical-free environment may be able to achieve. Such outcomes are different in nature from the result of a prescribing physician's effect on a willing patient. A way must be found to make them possible or the physician will not become a psychotherapist.

A second experience taught me more about limits. This patient was an eighteen-year-old girl, who had been given to bouts of agitated behavior throughout her life. Access to an automobile at sixteen had enlarged the arena of action: she had repeatedly been held in custody for reckless driving, had been extracted from the wreckage of her mother's car with a crowbar, and scarred by a fire she playfully set while going one hundred miles per hour up the California coast. She was a very attractive green-eyed girl with long auburn hair. Always distracted, chewing gum and tapping her fingers, she had a peculiar preference in clothing. She wore only white.

My supervisor for this case was a psychoanalyst who urged me to forgo drugs. I wanted to follow his advice, but in so doing I encountered opposition from the ward personnel who had to deal with her around the clock, and from the ward psychiatrist. The diagnostic problem was to differentiate mania (which would be treated today with lithium) from a manic defense against basically nonpsychotic problems. I decided to proceed without medication.

My patient, Linda Clark, communicated in bits and pieces, and usually only if I questioned her incessantly.

"Where were you born?"

"Back east."

"Where, exactly?"

"Midwest."

"What state?"

"Michigan."

"What city?"

"Around Flint."

"Can you tell me about your parents?"

Fidgeting, snapping of gum. "That's a cool necktie, Doctor. Salvation Army type, no?" Slight smirk on a face that was usually sad and blank. The agitated gum-chewing jaw gave it a spurious effect of liveliness. When I could think of her sadness, through a process of inference which competed with her behavior, there seemed to be a calming effect on both of us. I began to think that I was seeing a baby there in the guise of a young woman.

"You don't want me to care about you, do you, Linda?"

"Go fuck yourself," she said. I thought immediately of my supervisor, arming myself by remembering him. He had speculated that her preference for white showed a desperate expression of innocence or surrender, something virginal.

"You wear white because you really don't know anything about life at all. You are confused by what happened to you. White shows how innocent you are." I was reacting from hurt. I was exceedingly hostile.

She stood up and knocked over the chair. "I'm leaving."

"No, you're not," I said. "Pick up that chair and sit down. You'll leave when I tell you to leave and not a minute sooner." I was in a small office with no window. When I stood up, I felt that I filled the room. And she was a short girl.

She started to kick the wall, harder and harder. "Stop it," I said. "Just stop." Now I was furious. She must have seen it, and became quiet. Still her face was impassive. "All right, Linda," I said, "but we'll continue tomorrow." I rang for an attendant to take her back, and when they left I looked down the corridor, to see her slouching alongside him toward the waiting ward.

My supervisor encouraged me to persist, which I did. In the therapy sessions, I was looking for any way in which she might cooperate. I began to lose whatever contained stance I had tried to achieve. Islands of intuitive contact were demolished by the skillful theatrics of her disruption. I was bewildered.

As this feeling intensified, she allowed me to see some of her own helplessness, in brief moments when her face became lifelike and perceptibly sad. She revealed an extreme tiredness, as if to imply the loss of all the energy she had been squandering in the interests of distance. But shortly, when this led to a sense of mild hope in me, she would stub out a cigarette on the surface of my desk or open the door to leave.

I became more rigid. I dreaded the daily hours with her, and the nurse's morning report, as she reviewed the behavior of the patients overnight. Inevitably, Linda was the source of an incident.

Then she ran off. I worried about suicide or an accident, and was distracted from my duties. Three days later, the police found her in a desert town to the east, asleep under a neon motel sign. Her parents were irate and accused the hospital of gross incompetence. They transferred Linda to another facility. They said we were lucky they had decided not to press a malpractice suit.

In the conference held to go over the case, it was generally agreed that this agitated girl should have been calmed down with one of the major tranquilizers. After five months of residency, I was thrown into doubt about my competence. Where, I wondered, was the skill I thought I would rapidly develop? What good did all my reading do me? How could my supervisor have been right, when this was the outcome?

My discouragement began to lift when another patient of mine responded unexpectedly to a spontaneous and almost meaningless remark. The man, suicidal after the death of his wife, told me how he could not bear to sleep alone, how he awoke at 4 A.M., out of a dream, terrified, unable to care for his own needs.

"Yes," I said, "sometimes it must seem that morning will never come."

He was silent. "I doubt I'll be able to make it," he said.

And he told me about other times, earlier, during his marriage, when he had felt similarly, and then, in the next few sessions, about childhood incidents of hopelessness. I just listened. The material put me in a position to think about him. I started to read about depression, and discussed the subject with my supervisor. I was beginning to see something very simple: that to listen well, without trying to interpret, is a primary therapeutic mode.

In retrospect, I could also see that I had bitten off too much with Linda Clark, that one at my stage probably needed to use a drug to make therapy possible with someone as out of control as she. I could also begin to see that one must listen carefully and calmly before intervening with one's brand of help.

8.

PSYCHIATRIC RESIDENCY:
SECOND YEAR

After a year on the wards, the resident customarily turns to treating outpatients. Not in need of the controls and round-the-clock attention that inpatients are, they can usually co-operate better, and for that reason require a somewhat diff-erent set of skills. The place of psychotherapy in the treatment process, by itself or in combination with medica-tion, is usually greater. The dramatic turnarounds one sees with the acutely psychotic are less likely, and a finer under-standing of the therapy process becomes necessary. The resi-dent comes to his outpatients with a year of seasoning be-hind him, and can do without the trappings of the physician better than he could at the beginning of his training.

The notion that in psychotherapy people are subtly co-erced into change is revised by the sort of experiences I described in the last chapter, but tends to return until the therapist has undergone a period of his own treatment. Al-though he learns from every experience, his ability to reach a deep understanding of a patient depends on having him-self been understood in depth.

He doesn't know this then, or admit the necessity of an analysis, even if it is in the plans. Certainly it isn't *immedi-ately* necessary. The patients are right there to be treated. One gets help from supervisors. And improvement appears to come about. But how to judge its significance? He tends to assign permanence to the merely transitory. Soon, reversals belie what had seemed so established. In the end, it will be necessary that the therapist have the analysis or the intensive therapy experience. It need not be an accompaniment of residency training, when it is often inconvenient because of time and expense, but a genuine absorption in the attempt to understand people will make it an obvious and eagerly anticipated undertaking.

There's a potential for a split between what you tell yourself to be true, that you are really learning how to conduct psychotherapy, and a deeper suspicion that you are a fraud. The methods you learn may be useful, but the subject of human emotional life is too vast to yield to any method. The feeling of inadequacy becomes less and less acceptable as the years of training pass. Without the underpinning provided by learning the truth about your own development and how you are constituted, the training process is somewhat mechanical and strained. The division between I (therapist) and you (patient) is too sharp, and what you understand does not arise organically out of a comfortable awareness of how you are being affected by the patient. You tend to resist being affected in proportion to the strength of your own unanalyzed defensive systems and the extent to which the patient's problem touches them. This is the state of mind which accompanies the belief that therapeutic change is something one person *imposes* on another.

With Linda Clark I had wanted to evaluate my skill as a therapist. It seemed necessary to leave drugs out to learn the truth, which proved to be that in such an instance, my powers were insufficient. When you try to do without one kind of support, you have to find another. This is true not only in the beginning of a career, as I found with my patient, but later, when you are confronted with a case that challenges your conventional approach.

I recently treated a man of Italian background who was deeply depressed and was unable to tell me what was passing through his mind. I sensed that he could not and would not bear long silences from me. We gradually found our way toward a therapy that was marked by ordinary conversation, but we did this while still paying attention to his dreams, which he was willing to report, and to the connections between his early experiences and his symptoms. Without telling him anything of my personal life, I met his needs by relaxing the usual rules in psychoanalytic psychotherapy. We discussed his problems here and there among conversations about the news and especially his opinions of Americans as compared to the Italians he knew and loved. This led us to examine his sadness at losing touch with his roots. I searched my mind to explain his enthusiasm for his treatment and the fact that he was getting better. Should I consider it a sham and force him to confront my silence? Should I think of it as temporary support, relieving him of an acute condition but with no long-term implications? Or should I submit myself to an inexplicable process of helping, and admit that I couldn't tell where it was going to lead? I took a certain amount of pleasure in being flexible, and in being able to pursue an intuitive course. His depression lifted. Three years after his year of therapy, it hadn't returned.

In striking contrast to that good experience was one I had with an outpatient in my second residency year, Charles Covello, age forty-one, an engineer, who could not progress in relationships with women. He was unmarried and without social confidence. Also of Italian descent, though raised in this country, he was deeply and passively attached to his mother, and an only child. His father had been a model of passivity himself. The patient had a mathematical aptitude that bordered on genius. He skipped two grades and entered a famous technical university at the age of fourteen. His emotional development was retarded, however, and he had never managed to have a long-term relationship with a woman. The women would drift away because of his passive attitude, or he would get so dependent and demanding that they would have to eject him from their lives.

Mr. Covello applied for treatment in our clinic and was screened by the intake team, which found him to be non-psychotic, cooperative, and motivated. They pronounced him suitable for a second-year resident, and he was assigned to me.

He came with a good deal of written material. The interviewer and the psychologist prepared summaries of their findings which were intended to orient me. I eagerly devoured the information, and tried to put together a picture of his inability to get close to a woman without reproducing the tie to his mother. I was uncomfortable without some data to support my approach to the patient. This was how it was done, and, as a learner, I wanted to do the same.

I assumed I needed a system, an order. The typed summary told me, in typical medical fashion, about chief complaint, present illness, past history, family history, mental status, physical examination, psychological testing, formulation, diagnosis, recommended treatment. When I approached Mr. Covello, sitting in a chair in the large outpatient waiting room, I saw a short, balding man with dark brown eyes, and a soft, pleading expression, puffing the end of a cigarette. A handkerchief end hung out of the right front pocket of his trousers, making him seem careless. He had a thick mustache. I introduced myself to him, shook his hand, and led him to my office.

He was soft-spoken, quiet, shy, and as he told me his story there were long silences as he stared beyond me. I found myself asking him questions to speed up the flow of information. I was still, to an extent, the intern getting an efficient history when time is short, but time was no longer short.

It was difficult to get a straightforward account of his

problem, and his hopelessness, which should have been obvious, was obscured by my effort to get data. Instead of empathizing with his having to give someone the story of his life after having done so several times already, I simply asked for more facts. His depression was an obstacle to the collection of data, so we were opponents, in a sense, at the very outset. It was as if the formulation of a history, which I could then dictate and present to my supervisor, were the most important function of this first meeting. It would have been preferable, I think, to have let the conversation drift, to observe what he would choose to say and how he chose to say it, and to infer from such behavior what sort of person he was. But taking this approach requires confidence and a developed point of view toward such sessions, and is not generally encouraged in residents.

There are two schools of thought on the subject of first encounters or diagnostic sessions. One emphasizes observation, spontaneity, no routine to follow; the other, more traditional approach attempts to make an evaluation by covering the significant areas. It can be argued that one should know, for example, whether the patient has been hospitalized for mental illness, and might *not* learn this unless the relevant question is asked. This seems sensible, yet it might be more revealing to see this fact emerge in a spontaneous context, along with whatever feelings are associated with revealing it. What does the patient choose to avoid? Not that Mr. Covello had been hospitalized for emotional problems. He *had* had a year of treatment for tuberculosis in a sanatorium in Arizona, at the age of twenty-three, and I wouldn't have found this out without my thorough line of questioning. But with months of therapy ahead, it would have been preferable to dispense with such information gathering and take a more relaxed approach.

There was an unshaped, ineffectual quality to Mr. Covello which contrasted with my effort to be efficient, and on this contrast the attempt at therapy turned. Listening to tape recordings of our sessions, I can see I was probably trying to show by the example of my own behavior how he might change. If he could become less ineffectual he might be able to overcome the problem with women. On the surface, I was patient, but my tone of voice showed irritation with his long pauses, his yawns, and the grammatical slips that went uncorrected.

I tried to hold his depression at bay by concentrating on details. There were many clues that could have been construed to indicate that he was reproducing the bond to his mother everywhere he went. What he presented was an extreme ambivalence, an invitation to confusion rather than an opportunity for a relationship. I would have had to become conscious of the confusing effect on me of his behavior in order to generate useful comments, but my defenses required that I avoid feeling confused. With further experience, the therapist can permit himself to know how he is feeling without sacrificing his poise, and then can focus his remarks on the here-and-now fantasies and behavior, which will have convincing implications for outside life.

The resident can benefit from learning to impose silence on himself as protection against giving in to a sometimes uncontrollable urge to intervene, or to ask repeated questions. The need for self-discipline is acute, and silence will help. He will be surprised to observe turns of thought that are not available when he talks. He will gradually learn to afford himself this indispensable background for reflection.

After six months of treatment, Mr. Covello met a woman with two young sons. After dating her for a month, he announced that they were getting married. I was alarmed that he had jumped ahead to marriage. He explained that both of them were in their forties and wanted to build a life together, that they didn't have the time of younger people, and that they were in love. He attributed his success to the help I had rendered. I felt uneasy.

When I voiced my doubts to my supervisor, a man who was seemingly unencumbered by convention, he asked me why I was so concerned. Here was a virtually crippled man who had found someone to love. Who was I to impose my own ideas about marriage on him? I doubted that my previous supervisor would have seen it this way. He would have noted immediately the potential for disaster in an impulsive act, a bid by the patient to leap over lifelong, deep pathology into a seemingly normal life, which couldn't possibly work. Yet I found something liberating in my present supervisor's view. He had advised me once to tell a patient who was chronically late that I would lock the door after a set number of minutes. I had done this and found the patient on time after that. How invigorating it was to cut through the long, relatively static period of making interpretations.

I tried to persuade myself that Charles Covello was doing well, though it was disconcerting that his fiancée had recently been divorced for the third time. He presented an attitude of almost beatific peace with his new love, able to overlook all. Her name, Anna, was the same as his mother's, and an attempt to get him to examine the significance this might have for him was of no avail.

Four months after the wedding, he was again living alone. His wife had not been faithful. Two weeks after that he was brought to the emergency room in an aspirin coma. Charles Covello's easygoing ways, even his seemingly endless patience with his own struggle to find a woman, were finally perceivable as a facade for suicidal despair.

I began to think about how patients might try to please the therapist by seeming to improve, yet be so estranged from their own uncertainty that they would, in fact, be worse off. But how was one to judge? The key was in being able to know when you were insisting upon change for the sake of your self-esteem. And the only way you could arrive at this awareness was through the kind of extended study of yourself you can get only in a personal analysis.

I continued to treat Mr. Covello as an inpatient, and with his despair now out in the open, I did not have a difficult time discussing it. We talked at length, finally, about his sense of imprisonment in the infantilizing spell of his mother, and of his ambivalent urge to cling to and repel the women in his life.

After three weeks, he left the hospital and resumed outpatient treatment. I saw him twice a week for the next year. He managed to maintain a casual relationship with a woman for several months. He was able to acknowledge a feeling that he would never be able to overcome the pull of the relationship to his mother. Some of the apathy disappeared and I had the feeling that the disastrous attempt at marriage had brought him into the real world. Perhaps his premarital optimism derived from the belief that he had thought and talked long enough, that action, even misguided action, was what was required to break out of a paralysis of the will. This might also have been the basis for the appeal to me of my supervisor's attitude, but it was a dangerous one.

Mr. Covello's skills as an engineer led to a particularly good opportunity in the Seattle area. He decided to take it, and his therapy with me terminated. He later wrote to say that he had found another therapist. He kept in touch, with an occasional note, but gradually dropped out of sight.

Three years later Mr. Covello called to say that he was visiting Los Angeles and wanted to see me. He walked into my office with a springier step and a more forthright way of speaking than he used to have. Within five minutes I could see some of his old discouragement, but he evidenced a certain reconciliation to his ongoing need to keep working at his problems, instead of minimizing them. There was no false note of optimism. I felt respect for his courage.

He had a relationship with a widow who lived on a farm just outside Seattle. He loved the weekends in the country, and said that the physical work he did on the farm was helping him to overcome the effects of the lopsided development of his intellectual life, which had contributed to a chronic embarrassment in the world of relationships. Mr. Covello was becoming more of an integrated man.

As he stood up to leave, I felt a pang of loss. I shook his hand and told him how glad I was that his life had taken a turn for the better, and how very pleased I was to know him.

9.

PSYCHIATRIC RESIDENCY:

THIRD YEAR

By the time he starts his last year of training, the resident usually knows what career direction he wishes to take. He will go on to private practice or try to continue in hospital staff work, perhaps by starting with an extra year as chief resident, with its variety of teaching and administrative duties. Perhaps he will apply for a fellowship in such subspecialties as child or forensic psychiatry or become associated with a research team. He might choose to work in a mental hospital for a while. He makes such decisions in the light of a growing perspective on the field as a whole. He rounds out his training with experience on services considered vital to the education of a psychiatrist. Among these are neurology and psychosomatic medicine, which is commonly studied on the consultation-liaison service. The resident provides opinion and advice to house staff on the hospital wards, and thus renews contact with nonpsychiatric patients. At the same time, long-term therapy with selected outpatients provides an opportunity to appreciate the complexities of this work over time.

My own third-year experiences included an elective four months at the Hampstead Clinic in London, a center for treating children and training child psychoanalysts, where I attended numerous research conferences but was not permitted to deal with patients. Without analytic training, I was not considered ready. I went there for the adventure of learning from Anna Freud, who directed the clinic, and I was not disappointed. It was she who granted permission for this first instance of admitting a psychiatric resident as an observer. The opportunity to listen to the deliberations of men and women of extraordinary talent and dedication left a permanent effect on me. The research groups, consisting of six or eight analysts, met weekly, read relevant literature, discussed it in detail, kept minutes of every session, which were discussed in the subsequent one, presented case material carefully, and generated numerous interesting ideas in the process. Sometimes one or two members would write papers, always thorough and interesting. I appreciated the few direct contacts with Miss Freud herself, including one in which she tendered me the astonishing invitation to spend as much time as I wished in her father's Maresfield Gardens office, alone, looking at his antiquities, his books, his furnishings, and tasting the ambience of that historic room. This act of trust and generosity toward one still standing outside the door of psychoanalysis was a landmark in my life.

The period at the Hampstead represented the psychoanalytic future of my work, but a paper I wrote in the months before I left for England represented its present phase. Every resident had to present a paper in the third year. I chose to write about three patients whose therapy I had found it necessary to terminate, because they were not making sufficient efforts on their own behalf.

One was a gambler who couldn't stay away from Las Vegas, another a hysterical woman who repeatedly cut her wrists, and the third a young man who burglarized homes in his neighborhood. In each case, excellent progress in therapy had made me think that there would be a good outcome, but the patients nevertheless continued their ways. After using whatever capacity I had to understand and interpret these recurrences, to no avail, I finally threatened to terminate treatment if they didn't cease. In each case, the patient put me to the test, and I had no choice but to terminate. All three were shocked by my action, ceased being self-destructive, and eventually applied for a resumption of treatment, which recommenced on a more serious basis, and without further incident. I had been able to get them to control their compulsive behavior.

My paper was a portrait of striving for a serviceable point of view with which to conduct psychotherapy. My lines of reasoning were of two types, the analytic and what I chose to think of as the practical. I was stimulated by the philosophy of the supervisor who advised locking the door on people who came late. He suggested ways of dealing with actions in patients with character disorders. These patients do not feel conflict about their symptoms, because they have integrated them into their lives. The therapist doesn't have the advantage of addressing conscious conflict, so he has to find a way to generate conflict, to make the symptoms "ego dystonic." In my cases, an action instead of an interpretation was finally used as a reply to another action. If I couldn't make the effective interpretations which would arouse the necessary anxiety, and found that I cared more about the self-destructive effects of my patients' actions than they did, I had at my disposal the action philosophy of my unconventional supervisor. I could terminate.

I reviewed the pertinent literature and put together a presentation that was well-received by the staff. It recommended strength and decisiveness. In a way it was the behavioral equivalent of a drug. And it worked. It suppressed the symptoms.

Above all, it took account of my limitations. I could put an end to confusing, ineffectual treatment, and call it therapy. I could say that enough is enough. Fifteen years later, a depressed patient told me that she carried a gun. She was a compulsive, tense woman, with darting eyes and a marked tendency to deride herself without just cause. I had the feeling that I could be of decisive help to her, but in the matter of the gun, I said that I wouldn't see her if she kept it. I thought she had disposed of it, but two years later the issue resurfaced. A period of renewed severe depression brought the gun back from oblivion. When I learned that she still had it, I told her that she had to get rid of it, or we would terminate. She pleaded with me, saying that she had to have a means of ending her unhappiness if all else failed, that she couldn't bear the time psychotherapy takes without the reassurance of a personal solution. But I remained adamant and we terminated.

In response to her brief note of thanks for my help, I wrote back to say that I continued to be concerned about her and that if she could do without the gun, we could resume. Six months later, she complied. An unexpected surge of change marked the start of this next period of treatment. The fragmentation that had condemned this brilliant woman to a life in a dilapidated apartment clearly declined. She suddenly found that she could read, after a ten-year hiatus, and became aware of activities she enjoyed. I had taken the view that all we were doing was in the service of living, and that if she chose to reserve the right to die in the midst of it, then I wouldn't want to give freely of myself.

But this treatment would not have worked if I had known only what I knew as a resident. I had to have a much more advanced grasp of transference and resistance, of myself and my own genesis, to do the fundamental interpretive work that gave force to my threat to terminate. It is never a single technical maneuver that really makes the difference.

10.

THE BEGINNING
OF PSYCHOANALYTIC
TRAINING

It's good to be able to work alone for a while before starting yet another training program, though some prefer to begin analytic work during residency. I spent a year working with disturbed children in a state mental hospital, learning from the dedicated director, who brought intelligence and compassion into the otherwise barren reaches of custodial care. Meanwhile I began a small private practice, borrowing the office of a friend in the evening. When there were a sufficient number of patients, I opened my own office. I enjoyed the autonomy and freedom of being a full-fledged psychiatrist. It was interesting to consult with other physicians, and to be available for those patients whom more established practitioners tended to shun, such as the acutely disturbed, the psychotic, referrals from the juvenile court, people who couldn't get to the office. I went to local hospitals to see patients for consultation, with a confidence that came from having done this for several months in the hospital where I had trained just the year before. One afternoon, I agreed to see a man of twenty-two who was holed up behind a locked door at home. He had lost both legs in an automobile accident at the age of seven. His embarrassed father let me in. The two of them lived alone in a small duplex apartment, the mother having died soon after the accident. The young man and I talked across the barrier of the door. I sat on the floor, imagining what he might look like. I came to the house three more times in the following week, until he finally let me in. He was a fine-looking fellow. I was surprised that he could smile rather readily. The smile was possible, I thought, because he had had seven good years before his accident. He couldn't cope with his outrage at the hand fate had dealt him. I saw him on and off for ten years after that, providing bits of help at critical junctures. He made slow progress in his search for appropriate work, but there was a special poignancy in his difficulty in finding a suitable girlfriend. It was heartbreaking to see him having to be contented to daydream about the relationships other young men take for granted. This problem continued as long as I knew him.

One woman I treated was hospitalized for refusing to eat. I advised her physician that she be force-fed. (As a resident, I had seen such a move made with a similar patient.) She decided to eat. She then came to see me in the office, but lost weight again, falling to eighty-five pounds. I threatened to have her committed to a state hospital. This was the use of the power of the physician once again, the new practitioner flexing his medical muscles. But she did eat. She was a woman with a dual personality who, six years later, in the throes of real change, tore out bits of her hair after every good session. She eventually found freedom from the torment of childhood experiences of rejection and extreme hardship, and subsequent devilish treatment at the hands of her conscience. Hers is one of the therapies of which I am proudest.

These were cases for which my residency work had provided a start. I continued to see both patients through the period of my analytic training, and learned as I went. But there were others, less dramatically disturbed, with whom I had great difficulty. A nineteen-year-old girl had a stubborn streak which made her inaccessible to parents and teachers.

Her grades were far below her potential and she was frightened of boys. I worked with her twice a week, and saw her parents occasionally, as was my habit with child and adolescent cases, trying to combine a process of understanding with practical suggestions. The girl made slight progress over the course of eight months. It was unsatisfying for both of us, and she gradually lost interest in therapy.

I was able to help certain patients, sometimes, without knowing quite how. A twelve-year-old boy with a school phobia gradually became able to attend school, for reasons that escaped me. His therapy was an opportunity for discussion of his problem without pressure, which must have eased a tumultuous situation that featured a scene every morning, when either he wouldn't leave his room or his home, or he would jump off the school bus before it moved. His parents were divorced and his father lived in another country. The boy had an unusually vivid imaginary friend. I didn't see then that he was actually psychotic. Years later, he came to me with an overt schizophrenic breakdown. He recovered from that too, but by then I could understand that he was chronically schizophrenic after all, and probably had been for years. Even though I helped him, I lacked the conceptual tools with which to guide my interactions and to understand his situation. I was filling in the gaps in my residency training with experience and reading, but did not go home each evening with a sense of satisfaction, the way I did years later, when the work of deep comprehension became a reality.

After a year in practice, I could afford analysis and applied for training. This was yet another educational beginning, after college, medical school, internship, and residency, and one might think that it would be discouraging to find oneself starting all over again. But because of the fine focus of analytic thought, its very lack of eclecticism, and because the seminar groups were so small and scholarly, it was actually a welcome draft of fresh air.

There were two institutes in Los Angeles that came under the aegis of the American Psychoanalytic Association. Most of the major cities in the country have at least one such institute. I knew about the history of schism in psychoanalysis, beginning with the expulsion of Jung and Adler, but that was long ago and irrelevant. The presence of Jungian societies was a matter of no notice, let alone moment, and Adler was ignored. Freudian psychoanalysis was taken to be the only legitimate form, and only organizations that were part of the American were worth knowing about. What I didn't know at that time, as I tried to enter the psychoanalytic world, was that factionalism had been a reality throughout psychoanalytic history, and affected the workings of the institute I chose. How vitriolic and unamenable to reason feelings among colleagues could become! The conflicts were a feature of professional life on all levels, from local training facilities to national and international organizations.

I applied to the institute that had the reputation at the time for taking psychoanalysis more seriously. The most famous member of the other, Franz Alexander, had developed a kind of therapy known as the "corrective emotional experience." He deliberately took an attitude toward a patient that was supposed to compensate for the pathogenic attitude of the parents. For example, if the father had been harsh, he might choose to be soft and kind. If the father had been weak, he might behave strictly. Alexander wished to shorten the lengthy process of analysis this way, but I found his recommendations too much like stage acting. It wasn't what I was after. I wanted to learn how to search out the truth without playing roles.

Today, a young psychiatrist can apply to institutes of the American Psychoanalytic Association, or to one of the new institutes that accept mainly nonphysicians. There would seem to be no advantage in doing the latter, in my opinion, unless he is rejected by one of the more traditional institutes, because current training standards in the institutes of the American are very high. The training is demanding, and must be. It's part of the joy of the work that it calls forth one's best within a strict framework. The literary critic R. P. Blackmur wrote of how adherence to poetic form can "drag out" of the poet a level of expression that would never have come forth without the struggle to meet the demands of meter and rhyme. The same considerations apply to psychoanalytic work, in which the analyst's personal adherence to a method brings out his deepest insights and sets an example for the patient, who must struggle against his own defenses to face truths that are often painful. Analytic training aims to teach a definite technique, and not to be a leisurely or dilettantish sampling of various ideas. That is its great value.

The style of training varies among institutes. The New York Institute is known for its orthodoxy, its famous members, and its high standards. Janet Malcolm etches a sharp portrait of it in her book *Psychoanalysis: The Impossible Profession.* Chicago has a large, enterprising membership, including a sizable group of followers of the late Heinz Kohut, who founded an offshoot known as self-psychology. Pittsburgh, Cleveland, Seattle, have small, comfortable groups. Some institutes that are not part of the American, such as the William Alanson White group in New York, lean toward a view of analysis that emphasizes the interaction of analyst and patient, using some of the ideas of Harry Stack Sullivan, a psychiatrist who specialized in treating the psychotic.

An applicant who was repeatedly rejected by institutes of the American finally gave up and started his own. There is a growing number of new institutes that accept primarily Ph.D.'s. Numerous members of the American now teach in these institutes. Although this practice is frowned upon by the American Psychoanalytic Association, that group has not enforced a ban against it.

Those who found and operate the new facilities cannot be prevented from saying that they train psychoanalysts, because the title has no legal standing, though most members of the American would dispute the descriptive legitimacy of the word. New journals have begun to proliferate whose editorial boards are composed both of Ph.D.'s who are connected with the new institutes and MD's who belong to the American. So, too, with their contributors. Similarly, professional meetings have begun to feature discussions between leaders of the psychoanalytic establishment and analysts who are not affiliated with it. All of this bears the clear message that at least some independent analysts and institutes such as the New York Freudian Society and the William Alanson White Institute in New York have gained a measure of recognition and influence that has formerly been denied them. Moreover, after years of agonizing, the American Psychoanalytic Association is on the brink of admitting otherwise qualified individuals who are not psychiatrists to full training as clinical psychoanalysts. At the same time, it will retain its program for scholars who wish to have the advantage of a psychoanalytic education.

In our first seminar, a child analyst taught an overview of development one evening a week at her home. We five candidates found that our common devotion to the study of psychoanalysis made for a strong collegial bond. The seminar leader, a woman who knew many of the contributors to the field, gave us a sense of the historic dimensions of psychoanalysis. It was still young, as professions or sciences go, and many of its second generation of pioneers were alive. There were only a few thousand analysts in the world then. There are no more than seven thousand today—three thousand in the United States—a relatively minuscule number. If the sense of belonging to a tiny group, in which everyone knew everyone else, was a thing of the past, there was still a possibility of being familiar with a good many and of feeling solidarity in a common and arduous undertaking.

Each of us had begun a personal analysis. Most days of the week we were the beneficiaries of its careful observation, tact, and spareness of expression. The message from our analysts seemed to be: Be silent and think. Don't act impulsively. Don't barge in with poorly thought through ideas. Speak only when you know what you are talking about, and then be concise. This careful attitude dispelled confusion when it didn't paralyze us. Without knowing how our analysts decided how to behave on any given occasion, we could infer at a great distance a center of reflection, a point of view, which might someday be ours.

I marked up my copies of the major psychoanalytic periodicals,* moving from assigned papers to related ones, rereading many I had encountered years before, but anew, with eyes that were informed by the clinical experiences of residency and private practice. Nothing seemed to have been wasted. Patients who had not done especially well became suddenly interesting as examples of one concept or another. Yes, I could see now that the boy with the school phobia had employed the defense of denial in a way that suggested psychosis. He had been unwilling to face the fact that his father had moved far away and made no effort to stay in touch with him. His imaginary friend had a more vivid reality than most such friends do. I should have suspected something more dire than a neurotic process. Another patient's inappropriate action had demonstrated a response to subtle provocation by me, and I was able to admit to myself for the first time that I had wanted to suppress her ambition

---

*The following contain the major literature of the field: *The Journal of the American Psychoanalytic Association, The Psychoanalytic Quarterly, The Psychoanalytic Study of the Child, The International Journal of Psychoanalysis, The International Review of Psychoanalysis, Psychoanalysis and Contemporary Thought,* and *The Annual of Psychoanalysis.*

to be an actress, thinking that she probably had no talent, was extremely unattractive, and was only trying to make her husband and her mother angry by renting an apartment of her own. I had no business trying to take such a decisive role in her life, of course, but didn't realize what I was doing at the time. A third patient's phobia for bridges was an expression of her inability to sustain a relationship to her mother. Bridges meant relationships to her. The weak relationship to mother had undermined confidence in forming other relationships, and this flared up as a bridge phobia after an unsuccessful love affair. These were subtle bits of insight that began to flow from psychoanalytic education.

Along with the relevance of what we were learning, the rescuing of the past from oblivion inspired me. Illuminated by unexpected knowledge, the past took on a liveliness that it seemed to have lost. This was true both in our own training analysis and in our work with patients.

The patients would express their bewilderment with such thinking by saying something like: "The past is over, isn't it? Since it can't change, what's the point of spending all this time looking at it?" I would try to respond, knowing that whatever my reasoning, it would not be convincing without the actual experience of change. I would say that the value of looking into the past, mostly by reliving it in the controlled setting of psychoanalysis, is to understand it in a way one never could before. Out of this comes a better appreciation of the probable reality with which one had tried to cope, but which one had misread on the basis of the incomplete information of childhood and the dominance of fantasy. One begins to see without fear, and with a perspective that makes it possible for parts of oneself that had been suppressed to revive or to come into view for the first time. Newly conscious knowledge provides the means by which the patient can think about what is happening to him or get a grasp on the meaning of experiences soon after he has had them.

I was, of course, in the position of a patient myself in those days, not quite sure what this talk of psychoanalytic process really meant. But with my own growing experience of the surviving past, I would be able to follow these principles with increasing effectiveness.

The second part of this book contains numerous examples that illustrate this process.

11.

TRAINING ANALYSIS

The training analysis occurs in an educational setting, while the ordinary therapeutic analysis does not. The goal of institutes is to strive for conditions under which the training analysis will closely resemble the ordinary one. Most students of analysis bring to their training the neurotic conflicts of the "normal" person, and can benefit greatly from analysis, even if they are not flagrantly disturbed. The analytic situation mobilizes latent neurotic trends and generates an awareness of conflict that has been submerged. A student comes to see the ways in which his capacities to love and work have been compromised. Should he undertake the work as a mere technicality, and continue to believe that his analysis is just a way of fulfilling a requirement, his training will fail. Most students do not bring the sort of severe underlying pathology to their analyses that some ordinary patients do. At least, the admissions committees try to screen out the psychotics, borderlines, antisocial personalities, and applicants with perversions. Sometimes they don't succeed, and there are problems that may lead to dismissal in the midst of training. On a rare occasion, an individual with problems of an unusual sort goes on to demonstrate extraordinary talents, and may even become a major contributor. The criticism has been made that analytic institutes tend to screen out the more creative individuals, in favor of mediocrities who fall within the range of normal neurotic. There has always been a general fear of psychoanalysis as a process that destroys creativity by looking too deeply, and it's true that a psychoanalyst, by virtue of his power in the life of an exposed patient, can behave in ways that injure creative ability. Most analysts are deeply aware of their responsibility in this area. There's no way to briefly summarize the complexities of a process that is made up of so many convergent influences, but at least it can be said that severe psychopathology does not appear to be a prerequisite for creativity, even if many great artists have been quite disturbed.

In the institute where I trained, the students (called candidates then, and in recent years, clinical associates) could choose their own analyst, assuming the analyst was agreeable. I chose one of the more famous, one who wrote voluminously and well, seeing in him a model for my own ambition.

I quickly grew accustomed to his undivided attention and, lying on the couch in the quietude of morning, I spoke endlessly, almost without pause, filling the silence. It became a matter of conflict that he spoke so infrequently and that I seemed unable to be silent. I was supposed to say everything that came to mind, of course, and obeyed to the letter, but I wished, as the months and then the years began to pass, that I could have resisted this instruction, could have criticized him more openly for not speaking. I was obedient, as I had been obedient to my mother, and just as her emptiness had called forth from me an urge to fill her up, so I responded to my analyst. Yet I did not think of him as sad. It was, instead, as if he had an endless capacity for storing information and needed to know more, and still more, before he could say what I needed to learn. I told myself that I was helping him to function. He was, I could later appreciate, making it possible for a process to unfold. He was trying not to interfere with the spontaneous appearance of transference, the ubiquitous tendency to confuse the early figures in one's life with present ones. With the analyst out of sight and anonymous, the patient begins to develop an impression of him that is based on one or another of these key figures. This, then, gives access to the ways one felt in the past, through all stages of development. Within six months, against the background of my trying to help him to function, as I had tried to help my mother, came other phenomena. I was soon depreciating him, finding fault with his choice of clothing, with his writing style, with what I took to calling his narrowness. I was often slightly hurt when the end of the hour was announced. Thinking I could detect signs that he was irritated by my criticisms, by the decline of an initial period of idealization, I tried to control my resentment.

The institute itself was in the midst of change and my father transference became entangled in it. A generation of dissatisfied analysts was attempting to oust the old guard, of which my analyst was a distinguished member. During the Vietnam years, when rebellion was the common currency of youth, a group of men and women in their forties succeeded in opening the door for themselves as training analysts. Standards for selection were discarded in favor of a democratic point of view. It was thought that anyone considered a legitimate analyst ought to be able to analyze the candidates. The curriculum was revised in such a way that Freud's principles would be derived from case material, instead of introduced first as axioms. In addition, alternative theories, at first those of the Scottish analyst Ronald Fairbairn, and later, presented more vituperatively, those of Melanie Klein, began to capture the interest of a group of the dissatisfied. Discussion of these theories became emblematic of the deeper disgruntlement with mainstream Freudian thinking, itself a euphemism for the institute's old guard.

Many of the new ideas were exciting and deserved to be studied. Was it true, for example, as Fairbairn would have it, that babies are born with an urge for relationships, instead of wanting only to satisfy their drives (for food and sucking, for example), as Freud believed, of which the ensuing relationship to the need-satisfier was only an outcome? The idea of primary object seeking bespoke something better of man than Freud's theory did, a fundamental wish for relatedness, but there is no place for wishful thinking in the determination of truth. In any event, how could such an idea be tested? And what were the implications for analysis? If you began with an assumption of object seeking at the deepest level of motivation, didn't this change the whole tenor of the work, in the direction of uncovering the latent capacity to love in the patient? If one expected to find self-seeking without regard to the welfare of the object at the deepest level, didn't this become a search, instead, for the latent selfishness? Might not the different theories, essentially unprovable, appeal to different sorts of analysts, and serve as vehicles for the expression of a *personal* attitude toward life which preceded the pursuit of truth and the practice of analysis? And if this was the case, could a theory, as rationale, offer a given analyst a way to utilize his own deeply personal beliefs under the organization and aegis of a "scientific" point of view, a kind of theoretical justification for his own deeply rooted propensities? If so, how would this affect patients? Would it limit the range of any particular analyst according to criteria that might someday be specified?

A patient complained that her first analyst only emphasized penis envy. She felt that he had forced her to acknowledge that her career ambitions had been severely undermined because her deep aim was to attack the potency of the men whose jobs she wished to have for herself. Her second analyst believed that behind her argumentative character lay a woman frustrated by her mother's emotional unavailability in the first two years of her life. Attention to this as manifested in the transference (reactions to interruptions in treatment or lapses in the analyst's attention) generated the theory that her penis envy, which appeared in dreams and conscious fantasy, was secondary to early deprivation. The idea was that the penis became a symbol for what others had that she lacked, namely access to mother. She now felt understood, stopped being so disgruntled, and moved ahead in her career.

Another woman patient of the first analyst found that her life became greatly enriched as a result of analysis, and her achievements as a writer greatly enhanced. The same issue, penis envy, had played a major role in her treatment, but she did not experience a deep resentment of the analyst as a result of it. Did he behave differently toward her than he did to the first patient, though the subject was the same, or was she able to make better use of his interpretations for other reasons? Contrary to received tradition, therapeutic change in a patient is not sufficient evidence for the validity of the theory of the analyst who conducted the treatment. There are just too many factors that bear upon the experience of analysis to assign proper weight to all of them at this time.

In another direction, there was Melanie Klein's idea that fantasy life of a far more intricate and aggressive type than Freud had suspected dominated infancy, and, as a corollary, that far more primitive and aggressive fantasy dominated adult life as well. This coincided with my growing awareness of the powerful role of fantasy. To take a small example, it seemed to me that one's attitudes toward people could have the effect of changing their very appearance. Anger might make someone look vaguely unhealthy, either objectively or in the eye of the angry beholder. And it was clear that the way you dealt with a person was crucial to the way in which he manifested himself to you. Yet it seemed dangerous to think, as the Kleinians seemed to, that an analyst trained in their method could provide unsuspected meanings, one after another, while the patient unspooled his associations, as if a kind of magical mental braille were at the disposal of those in the know.

Having been befriended by one of the Young Turks who were in the process of overthrowing the old order, I studied these and other ideas with enthusiasm, and grew dissatisfied with my own analysis. It took a period of work before my analyst was able to elicit from me the hostility I was feeling toward him. The new ideas, which were so appealing to me, channeled my ambivalence into a seemingly impersonal realm, the world of theory, and for that reason they were an especially good covert vehicle for hostility.

The reliving of the relationship with my father brought to a high state of consciousness elements of the struggle against identification with him. I loved but depreciated him, wanting never to acknowledge his primacy, as if it stood in the way of my own development. A much maligned term and idea—castration anxiety—showed itself repeatedly rife with meaning. Dreams contained symbolism that showed my primitive urge to take something especially alive away from my analyst and, before him, my father. In proximity to such wishes were experiences of terror in which I myself became the object of such intentions. This was not easy to see clearly at first, for there were layers of defense against recognizing the outlines of the primitive world of a child's making.

Ever more aware of my dreams, therefore ever more able to remember them, I became more sensitive to those my patients brought as well. In the same way, having been witness to my analyst's ability to assign meaning to all sorts of seemingly minor communications from me, and to weave together interpretations that captured something essential, vital, and true, usually through an examination of the transference, I became an acute observer of the distortions my patients made of me, and I, too, tried to weave. Being appreciated as a complex expressive being, I could begin to appreciate others. I developed the patience to bear the misconceptions of me that patients presented, waiting for the right moment to set these in a context that would lead to insight.

Experimentation with the varieties of psychoanalytic ideas was a part of my activity. Sometimes it seemed reasonable to take one point of view, sometimes another. It depended on my mood, my newest reading, the state of the transference, and the patient. There seemed to be nothing systematic about it. The only thing that went on consistently, indeed relentlessly so, was my analysis. In this respect it was the prototype of continuity and integration, the spine of my education. I remember the stunning effect of reading a book by Melanie Klein called *Envy and Gratitude,* in which her genius manifested itself in a detailed explication of the infant's relation to the breast, where, in her view, the feeling of envy begins. Only later can a child feel grateful, instead of dominated by an urge to take without recognizing what is freely and lovingly provided. I saw support for aspects of this theory in myself and in my patients. Gradually, the preoccupation faded, leaving behind an abiding legacy of knowledge and awareness, while another new piece of knowledge flooded the subjects of my concern with light. Fairbairn's idea that a baby internalizes only to overcome unsatisfactory relationships proved fascinating. Theoretically, a perfectly satisfying childhood would result in no need to develop "internal objects," organized versions of one's parents and others, to which to cling. The implication was that the more satisfying the childhood, the more the individual's relations with others were unhampered by internal residues from the past, which made these relations more "real." I marveled at the innumerable ways in which the Oedipus complex led to all possible ratios of strength and neurosis.

The analysis gradually deepened into an ever-present background of preoccupation, with periods of anguish, as I regressed into what had survived of a child's struggle to make sense of his world. One day I felt a rush of anxiety which was only relieved when I could see, out of the corner of my eye, my analyst's foot as it rested on his ottoman. I had experienced the terror of an infant who was utterly alone. Later on, in a time that was measured in years, the analysis moved toward resolution when the principal elements had been understood well enough. I was grappling both with my own life's conflicts, and with the way in which these conflicts could becloud my judgment in the world of relations among analysts. It was a struggle to see clearly the compelling attraction that the rebellious coteries had for me. Subtle forms of bribery, such as referring patients to those who would join ranks in a group united on presumably theoretical grounds, became more and more clearly visible. Also, I began to take a skeptical view of the various waves of new ideas, as they swept, one after another, onto the abiding psychoanalytic shore. This was liberating. Yet this entanglement of theory and professional relationships did not invalidate theories. It was enough, I realized, to be a good analyst. One did not need to join a subgroup with revolutionary intent. There was room for all of us under the umbrella, where we could disagree to any extent, without violence to the whole and without sacrifice of individual development. I was witness to the effectiveness of the fundamental Freudian ideas, with their vast scope. Eventually, I would be able as well to admit of their limitations, but this in no way compromised the deepening grasp of their powerful essence.

The overt theoretical and personal struggles in the institute where I trained are not the rule, though they have been a feature of the development of psychoanalysis since its inception. Freud's early attempts to retain what he regarded as the proper direction for his work, by eliminating people like Adler and Jung, echo into the present day, where schism sometimes overtakes an existing group and results in the creation of two. This process occurred in Los Angeles in 1950, and has happened in a number of other American cities. The personal and the professional are easily entangled in the work of the analyst.

When my five years in analysis were over, I was in possession of a reflective ability that made most of life's ensuing vicissitudes amenable to deep contemplation. This was not perfect understanding, protection against catastrophe, or proof against the human condition. And it was available not at once, but haltingly. Difficult periods were accompanied or followed by a dream that lent perspective. Unresolved aspects of development could continue to be studied. The analysis was not a final configuration, but a comprehensive framework which could yield to pressing evidence for enlargement and amendment. The sense of a reasonable line of development, of the connectedness of all elements, yielded wholeness; again, this was not an inhumanly static achievement but a repeatedly attained state, enriched by the inevitable regressions and recoveries that are the hallmarks of all stages of life from infancy on.

Given a single such experience, one must extrapolate a good deal to form an opinion about the best choice of training analyst. I speak from a base of a good experience in a specific situation. An ideal training analyst, besides being humane, would, I think, combine scope and depth without adherence to a narrowly defined school of thought. Such an analyst is not blind to new developments but will not discard the body of analytic thought for a captivating but unproved theory. Eclecticism in the analyst is unlikely to lead to an integrated personality in the patient, for its spirit is one not of continuous striving for consistency but of the acceptance of dissociation between contradictory points of view. There is a necessary tension in the analyst's effort to acknowledge the value of a variety of viewpoints while patiently trying to integrate them with his basic orientation. This tension comes of a fundamentally scientific spirit and not the collection of diverse hermeneutic meanings.

Some think that an easygoing analyst might be best for a rigid student, or vice versa, but this is Alexander's "corrective emotional experience" in disguise. What counts is intellectual range, tempered by compassion, and a capacity for sustained inference from what is expressed by the patient to the depths which underlie it. But the problem is: how can you tell who has these qualities? You are left with reputation, published papers, the advice of others, and most of all, personal opinion to go on. It's indispensable to discuss potential analysts with anyone who has had experiences with them, and to compare what various people have to say. After a while, make appointments with those who appear to be real possibilities. It is wise to take several sessions in which to gather impressions before setting out on the long work of analysis, and it is always the prerogative of a patient to terminate if, later on, he finds his analyst seriously deficient. Even though you know ahead of time that analysis takes many years (perhaps five on the average), and that there are bound to be periods of discontent, you don't relinquish your continuing right and responsibility to judge the nature of the experience, and to act on your own behalf when you need to. Critical feelings toward the analyst may be the result of negative transference, and are best analyzed. But not every criticism is based on transference. There are moments when a patient will have to decide which it is and take appropriate action.

12.

SUPERVISED

ANALYSIS

The three essential elements of psychoanalytic training are the personal analysis, seminar study, and supervised work. Doing analysis and being a patient in analysis at the same time vitalizes your understanding of patients because you can put yourself in their place. This is a necessary corrective to the physician's tendency to sharply separate himself from his patient from the start and thereby curtail the key process in which the boundaries of the relationship blur and clarify.

My own preoccupations with competing theories led me to seek out supervisors whose views were at variance with one another and with those of my own analyst. I wanted to hear all the rationales from which I thought I might be able to discern the elements essential to good work. What experiences in residency had begun to teach me was to be continued and developed in analytic training: that people of different viewpoints appeared to get results and also fail. This inconsistency per se did not nullify the potential pertinence of their theoretical points of view, but it did call attention to the fact that it was always a living person who was conducting analysis, not a robot trained to high tolerances in a given school of thought. Since it was a person, perhaps there was something personal about what worked. I thought the data on which the theory of technique was based were incomplete without fuller attention to the person of the analyst.

I did not wish to be captured by a theory, nor did I wish to float forever in an eclectic backwash. I saw from observation of others as well as myself that a web of rationalization based on personal conflict can confuse supposedly scientific considerations. It was a glaring fact, akin to the emperor's nudity, that analysts of different temperaments seemed to recommend technical stances that rationalized their personal dispositions. Or they attached themselves to theories that might make up for a deficit, the disorganized embracing a rigid technique, the cold of heart trumpeting the virtues of empathy.

I had five supervisors. My first was a rather colorless but likable man, with an uncanny ability to organize material logically. He was of no discernible school of psychoanalytic thought, and there was no conflict in listening to him. I would present my data week after week and would come away amazed at what he saw that I hadn't. The most important thing I learned was that a patient's material can be seen from many points of view, but the one most likely to lead to sustained organization is that of the transference. Try to perceive evidences of the transference, he urged. I had been told this by teachers in my residency, and had read about it, but this kind man's words, in the context of dealing with an actual analytic case, made the idea really sink in. The fact that I was exploring the transference in relation to my own analyst also enabled my supervisor's words to take on new meaning. The patient whose treatment he supervised was several years my senior, the owner of a well-known restaurant in our area, and highly opinionated. It was strange to have a patient on the couch for the first time, and my interpretations sometimes echoed in my ears hollowly. The patient had a propensity for making belittling remarks to me as if I were his younger brother, who was the first person in his life whom he had belittled. My interpretations to this effect furthered the unfolding of the process. Nevertheless, he had extremely rigid defenses, which I could not adequately address, and at eighteen months of treatment, with minimal gains (he became slightly more able to form a bond with his wife), he terminated. Understanding something about transference is not a magic wand for change.

The second supervisor was an advocate of the ideas of Fairbairn. He came from the Southwest, and talked in simple, colorful language that dispelled some of the more arcane intricacies of analytic theory. He reminded me of the unconventional man who had supervised my work with Charles Covello, but he was more scholarly and careful. "Patients are all having the problem of growing up," he would say. "They don't know how." This summarized a great deal. And how refreshing to be told it without the usual jargon! He had retained the earthiness of life on the ranch, a cowboy analyst to put next to the stereotype of the overintellectualizing, introspective, nonphysical hermit in the darkened room. It was as if he could look up at the sky and forecast the weather. I presented material reconstructed from notes and he interrupted whenever he wanted. I never finished an account of the entire week. We'd get off into other realms. He recommended books, articles in journals, and writings in the literature of other fields.

I used to see him loping along the streets near his office for a noontime walk. Once I saw him standing next to one of my fellow candidates who was in analysis with him. The candidate was on a motorcycle, and they stood talking in an animated way at the curb as if such extra-analytic contacts were an ordinary thing. But they were not. Analysts tended to be almost as formal outside the office as they were within it. I liked the idea that the analytic relationship wasn't as fragile as it was made out to be. I asked myself whether this man's behavior as an analyst appealed to me as a contrast to the extreme discipline of my analyst, and I thought it did. But what was the meaning of the contrast? Was the appeal merely my own defense against the transference?

The consideration pressed itself on me: What are the conditions that would make the most of a given analyst's capacities? What are the conditions under which each analyst can exploit the full potential of his creative ability to understand another person? I knew that there was no easy way to sum up any one person's approach, and I had my own experience as a guide. I could be quite silent or talkative, depending on many factors. A voluble patient might evoke an urge to listen at great length. A patient's silence in the beginning might create a mood in which I would choose to speak carefully at intervals, and eventually grow silent as well. What was needed at a given time was decided by the patient's behavior, my grasp of his problem, and what I was capable of. If I knew something I thought the patient ought to know, I would usually say it. Otherwise, I would wait. Over the course of a whole treatment, I would behave very differently, depending on the patient and his or her problems. Some required and received a good deal of responsiveness, while others did better with much less talk. This wasn't based solely on diagnosis, with more feedback for the more disturbed. In ways I am not entirely conscious of, the meaning that the patient takes on for me, the countertransference valence, contributes to the kind of behavior I exhibit, whether I like it or not. I naturally hope to understand my behavior better and better, and be not so much mastered by it as able to determine what it will be. Yet always I reserve the right not to have to know ahead of time precisely why I act as I do in certain pivotal moments.

One patient was a twenty-three-year-old married woman, probably unsuitable for a candidate because of her tendency to act out problems rather than talk about them. After several months she got pregnant by a man with whom she was having an affair, and demanded that I write a letter recommending abortion. This was before abortions were easily obtained. I discussed the issue with my second supervisor, who urged that I take my time in understanding the request, not ruling it out immediately but not complying either. My Young Turk colleague actually advised that I refuse outright and tell her that psychoanalysis was more important than any individual person, that I would not besmirch it by colluding with her tendency to act without caution. He probably meant that the analyst does not deal with practical problems by giving advice or support. This was an instructive dichotomy of views. I could hardly agree with my colleague that psychoanalysis was more important than any particular person, much as I admired his commitment to the work. I tried to understand what was involved in the patient's situation, but at this point she could not bear to free associate. She repeatedly demanded action of me, which I refused to take, at least until I knew more about the meaning of her panic. This was insufficient for her and she quit.

My third supervisor was a talkative and charming person. The case we discussed, an inhibited man with examination anxiety, no self-confidence, but high ambition, turned out well. This was the first patient whose analysis I was able to bring to a successful conclusion. My supervisor had much to teach me about understanding patients. He was intuitive and open, while adhering to a basically traditional viewpoint. But the emphasis he placed on the analyst's reaching out to form an alliance with the patient made me think that he was giving his own ebullience a rationale for being integrated into his work. When he told me to tell the patient: "Let's look at this dream together," I sensed a point of view that was dissonant with my own. I thought it unproductive at the very least, but more, that a promiscuous togetherness of patient and analyst was implied. By being actively elicited, the spirit of cooperation was somehow unearned. I knew that others of more taciturn character were critical of this man's technical recommendations, and asked myself how much of their attitude was based on their own personal requirements. I felt free to tell him all this, and he took no umbrage at my remarks.

The fourth man was extraordinary in the skill with which he formulated data. He managed to focus on the material with a sharpness that intimidated me, as if whatever I could say of my own thought and technique was without value. The degree of discouragement made me suspect, after a while, that my reaction to him was one of displaced transference. It's often the case that a supervisor evokes responses in the student that more properly belong in his own analysis. Something of my fear of the penetrating insight of my analyst was being expressed where it didn't belong. The case was difficult, a middle-aged man with deep wells of hostility that sometimes became murderous. He moved with a gliding grace, spoke softly, unemotionally, always implying violence. He chafed at the conditions of analysis and finally moved out of town, with a promise of return that never materialized.

I then began to see a psychotic woman under the supervision of the same man, though not as a formal part of the analytic training program, for she was clearly unsuitable for analysis. I found that I needed to deal with her disconnected outpourings at such a rapid rate, coping with one set of statements after another with hardly a moment to think, that my weekly supervisory sessions were always far behind our sessions. Also, because I had to think on my feet with her, the scalpel-like insights of my supervisor were undermining my sense of adequacy. Fortunately, I was able to bring these experiences into my own analysis and to work toward understanding why I couldn't tolerate and learn from them.

My psychotic woman continued to batter me with an

endless line of chatter. Beyond a certain point, the effect was to make my mind wander. To stay with her, I needed to grasp a large form that could contain what she was telling me. I came to see that she was primarily projecting her confusion, getting me to feel it in order to obtain relief, and I made much of this bit of understanding to point out the pressure with which she was dealing. But interpretations of the content of her remarks were still generally of no avail. I felt continuously challenged to provide a context for both our sakes, but material from a given hour or week was superseded so quickly by what came next that it seemed useless to discuss it. I needed to talk about my own sense of being beleaguered, but whenever I tried to voice it to my supervisor, he acknowledged it with lip service only. So I would resume an account of the hours. I eventually came to the conclusion that he was too tempted to show how cleverly he could put together meanings from her material. This had the effect of undermining my already shaky confidence, as it ignored the cacophony in the messages with which I was faced on the spot. The supervisor was more an interference than a help, and I stopped seeing him.

My fifth, and last, supervisor was one of the Kleinians in our city. He formulated material with the unique Kleinian attention to ongoing primitive fantasy, and held me spellbound with a seemingly unending store of startling, stimulating insights. "I think he's attempting to get inside your mind and take control of your thoughts, like burrowing into the breast to get control of the milk," he might say, after I told him of my difficulty in sorting out some statements in a given hour. His vivid metaphor made sense to me. I did feel that the patient, a very bright engineer who was trying to climb a corporate ladder, had a sneaky quality to him, that he could be conniving and manipulative. He was essentially a compulsive man, and my approach, unfortunately, became equally compulsive. Difficult to treat, as such patients are under any circumstances, he appeared to make no progress, though I persisted for years in systematically applying the insights I was getting. Perhaps insight wasn't enough, I thought, knowing by this time that either this brand wasn't or insight in general wasn't, but still trying my best to put the principle to the test.

With other patients, these same ideas were to prove extremely helpful. Klein's concept of a depressive position, for example, became an integral part of my thought. The developing baby reaches a point in the first year of life when its anger against the frustrating mother meets with its love for the satisfying one, and fear of injuring the beloved causes a phase of concern for the mother, with efforts by the baby to give of itself in such a way as to make the mother feel good, to repair her, so to speak. Klein saw a relationship between these feelings of the baby and depression, both in childhood and later. That one might relive this conflict in a variety of adult situations, including analysis, was clear to me. But for the patient under supervision, neither this nor any other concept made any difference. The Kleinian approach, as taught by this supervisor at least, seemed too rigid, too all-knowing, inflexible.

You have to walk a line between getting the sort of consistent training that enables you to develop the necessary discipline to bear down over long periods with a difficult method, and the training that opens your eyes to the variety of approaches that provides flexibility and resourcefulness. The young analyst is in the process of using experiences to form a unique skill consistent with a unique personality. The passive absorption of vast amounts of new information is gradually succeeded by an active utilization of experiences in his own analysis, in supervision, reading, and treating patients. This leads to a more and more internally consistent and functional whole.

When my supervisory period ended, I found that I enjoyed the unaccustomed privacy. After having been a student all my life, there was now a spacious ease in my schedule. I was able to observe more closely than ever my own way of working. Sometimes a bit of writing or a conversation would contain, as if by accident, an arresting sentence, which would float to mind in the midst of a session. Or what I realized about one patient would become pertinent to another on the very same day. Or tiredness would lead me to the caution of silence, and, without the disturbance of interventions from me, unexpected turns in the patient's material. I would think: I have been too ready to speak; I must remember to be quiet more of the time. Or I would, almost without preparation, begin to speak and find myself saying more than I had suspected I knew, recognizing that I had *had* to speak to make it available to myself and the patient. I would learn my lessons, old ones and new, ever more aware of the magnetic tension between reason and imagination, not renouncing a line of thought because it was inconsistent with another, if an intuitive sense told me that it was possible that both were right.

There is another category of important teachers, shadow supervisors whose acquaintance one makes through their writings. In the treatment of my psychotic patient, I received support from reading the work of Harold Searles, a man who has dedicated his life to treating and writing about the treatment of the chronically psychotic. I needed to make contact with the principle that one is always groping, always misperceiving, and recovering, finding one's way toward moments of enlightenment. This forgiving attitude stands in contrast to waiting for the supposedly perfect moment, saying the perfect thing. It is a hazard of analytic training that you can develop a belief in the perfectibility of the method, as practiced in a session or throughout. In order to persist in the face of discouragement, you need to have it brought home to you, in a form you can use, that nothing is perfect, no matter what your skill. Searles, with his stories of struggle in the face of mountainous pathology, of failure and persistence, struck just the right note for me.

The work of D. W. Winnicott opened my eyes to innumerable vistas of thought. He was a child analyst who is best known for his concept of the transitional object, those soft toys or pieces of cloth to which small children grow so attached, and which they use to help them go to sleep, and which form models for creativity later on. The appeal of his writings is manifold, but the spirit is captured best in the idea that psychotherapy is a kind of play between therapist and patient, and that if play is not possible, that very problem becomes the primary focus of therapy. The word "play" suggests something undisciplined, but Winnicott's work was anything but that. His recommendations combined severe adherence to procedure with a receptiveness to spontaneity in the patient and himself, the very model of an integrated man in a field in which many practitioners seem withdrawn and rulebound.

Just as my supervisors and my analyst reappear in my thoughts at various moments in the conduct of my work, so does Winnicott. He is in some ways more of a construct of my own imagination, made out of what I glean from his writings. I've already mentioned that it's a very active process in the therapist which shapes experiences for various educational purposes. Reevaluation constantly occurs in the light of further experience. For example, I get a great deal more from my first, colorless supervisor, whose simple insights have stood the test of time, than I do from some of the supervisors who initially impressed me more. Searles means much when I am faced with a psychotic patient. Winnicott supports the play of my imagination. My own analyst reinforces relentless discipline and the deep generosity of effective work.

Freud abides above all, as a presence, the author of an immense oeuvre, the founder of my field. The facts of his life seen so many ways by so many biographers create an impression that shifts from the extraordinary man of soaring intellect and discipline to the humane clinician with his feet on the ground. And often, for me, there is the afternoon light in his Maresfield Gardens office, the view of his green yard in the waning months of his life.

13.

ONE'S

OWN VIEW

John Gardner has written of the "vivid and continuous dream" that guides the novelist and grips the reader. The intuitive psychotherapist is able to have an ongoing dream about his patient, which yields a similarly gripping continuity. The dream is both a given and an invention. It gradually appears as the patient's life is imagined by the therapist.

The organization of the therapist's pictorializations is the framework on which he hangs unfolding data, using memory and intuition economically to grasp continuities. He remembers easily because what he knows is tied together by the logic of inference.

The therapist's imagery is conjured as the patient describes. The patient's mother is selected from mothers he has known, seen, or read about. An idealized mother, for example, might suggest the mother in a Mary Cassatt painting, or the Norwegian immigrant in *I Remember Mama,* or the admired mother of a childhood friend, a motherly-looking woman seen once on a train, or a combination. Added information provides detail for the images, which become more concrete. All of this goes on without deliberate effort. It is just a way of actively responding. People, places, and scenes are all imagined this way.

At a point the therapist comes into possession of an intuitive understanding that yields more information than what was used to construct the image. At this time, he finds himself with new insights about the principal actors and scenes. His thought outpaces what he has been told.

The characters are alive. This is similar to the moment in the writing of fiction when the characters begin to dictate the action, and the author must attend to their demands. The therapist is having a kind of coherent dream of the patient's life, closely attuned to the reality as given. The interpretations that are derived from this dream facilitate the patient's freedom to imagine. This breathes life into the stereotyped past, which begins now to be reimagined. The patient takes up new points of view to explain his development.

The therapist may be surprised by a new detail, which is out of keeping with his version of the person or situation in question. He may have heard wrong in the first place, distorted the material presented by the patient, because of the power of his preconceptions. These are clues for a thought process, by which he can reexamine his prejudices or, perhaps, perceive that the patient is shifting the emphasis, in accordance with an evolving relationship to an important figure. The patient may have presented his father as beastly at first, more kind later, or vice versa. The dream is elaborated and revised.

In this way imagination forms a picture of reality, and one knows that "reality" deserves quotation marks, for what one searches out cannot be a phenomenological moment that exists apart from the context of the patient's personal experience, or free of his revisionist memory. One never emerges from the realm of experience into pure objectivity. One's advantage as a therapist is in knowing this and trying to take it into account at every step, working with the defenses toward a lessening of distortion, like panning for gold.

It was in a certain extended and concentrated teaching

situation that I first realized that my imagination was being put to use in a way which resembled that of the novelist. During four-hour sessions with twenty child therapists around a large table, in an atmosphere of courtesy and attentiveness, I applied myself to understanding the descriptions of cases. The stages were as follows: the presentation of initial descriptive data; the addition of details not included in the first description, always important; the appearance in my mind of one or more scenes in the patient's life; certain conclusions drawn by me from concentrating on the scene; discussions with the therapist which unearthed previously undisclosed information; and often a marked deepening of understanding.

For example. A therapist of obvious integrity and dedication speaks of a child entering her playroom, mother accompanying. The therapist is sitting at her desk. As the child comes toward her, she turns in her chair to face him. The mother hesitates at the door. The therapist rises, introduces herself to the little boy and his mother. The mother, only halfway across the threshold, turns to leave. The therapist is surprised at the speed with which the mother withdraws, and wants to invite her to stay, but is unable to speak. When mother has left, the boy stares anxiously at the door.

The therapist goes on to describe several hours, but I am preoccupied with this initial moment, when she wanted to speak but found that she did not. The child, I reason, might have felt similarly about his mother, prematurely abandoned. The case material supports this guess. Mother had been working since the child was six months old. He had been placed in a child care center all day, all week. Mother insisted on regaining her independence as soon after childbirth as possible, not because the family needed the money but because she seemed to have been threatened by the weight of responsibility for her child. This was well rationalized under the heading of women's rights. Father had protested against mother's wishes, and was able to drop in to see his son several times a week because he worked nearby. Now I imagine the six-month-old baby in the child care home.

I am also in the role of father looking in on the lost boy. By hearing this material, I am allied with his development, in favor of mending discontinuities.

The therapist expresses hostility toward the mother, indicating that she could never seem to come in for an interview. The boy is depressed, lonely, and has recently begun to pilfer candy at a local store, the apparent reason for starting therapy.

The store I imagine is the candy store of my own youth, with its amazing selection of good things in all colors and shapes, its confectionery smells, and the kind middle-aged woman who was in charge. I imagine the little white bags that are used to hold one's selections. I see a classmate of mine from second grade, blond and freckled, a lonely-looking boy, staring at the counter and reaching out for a roll of Necco wafers, a favorite of mine. No one is looking at him. An urge to steal is about to come upon him. I realize in my reverie that this boy was an adopted child. I remember that I had studied him carefully when I found this out, as if he were an abnormal child because of it. I could not express the depth of my sorrow that there was such a thing in this world as being adopted.

The therapist meanwhile continues a diatribe against the boy's mother, her coldness, her lack of cooperation. Now I notice something forlorn about the therapist, something sorrowful in her voice behind the attempt to express frustration. She protests against this mother, in full identification with her patient. She lacks a stable perspective with which to observe the entire clinical situation without bias. Suddenly, I think: She had been adopted.

I describe my reverie to the audience, speculating about the possibility of the child's having been adopted, without embarrassing the therapist with my guess about *her,* and I make a point of emphasizing that the case is vividly imaginable for me because of all the information the therapist has been willing to give. (In such situations, I always look for the good in the therapist's work, trying thereby to help him or her cope with the stress that is a part of open presentation of the very private events of a case, and I try not to abuse my privileged role as one who may comment at will on the work of another person, who bears ultimate responsibility.) When I stop, there is a silence, and then the haltingly given information which confirms my guess.

Now the supervision, enlivened by this personal element integrated with the material, and by an intensification of the reality of the work, advances into a consideration of the boy's play, which includes numerous references to adoption. The mother doll adopted the baby doll. The crocodile took pity on the ugly frog and adopted him. He was not an adopted child, but felt that he was. Perhaps his mother's attitude includes some form of denial that he was her biological son. This is enough for the moment. We are on the right track.

Two weeks later, the therapist reports that the mother has finally been interviewed, and has given the history that her own mother had died before she could remember, and that a stepmother had raised her and her brother. Probably the trauma of an early loss of her mother had induced distance from her own son, because she was threatened with the reliving of loss if she gave herself fully to him. I heard no more about the patient until the following year, when, at a similar conference, the therapist summarized her work to date. Mother had been willing to enter therapy herself and had become much warmer toward her son. The boy had been reenacting with his therapist his uncertainty about his mother's affections, gradually more able to express in play a sense of having been cheated of her love. Simultaneously, his stealing disappeared and he became more alert in school.

In Chapter One, I described how important details of my life were used as vehicles for thought about a patient's conflicts. Here, it is innocuous memory that contributes imagery which gives rise to usable insight in a supervisory situation. The characters in my own version of the drama came to life without conscious selection, in a state of unusual concentration. Four hours is a very long time to be focused on one case, and makes possible extreme continuity of attention and richness of imagery.

The same rigorous process applies to direct work with patients, I think, with protracted lengths of time required for a descent into the depths, and the fine tuning of one's own imagery. Instead of one scene, there are innumerable scenes, joined into an imagined reality that can bear the full weight of all information as it is disclosed or discerned.

The emerging unity of the patient's life originates in the imagination of the analyst as with the mother, who remembers the early events that the child could not, and imagines his possibilities in a world that is wider than he can know. *The analytic process permits the analyst to use his imagination in proportion to his fidelity to fact.*

PART II

THE PRACTICE

14.

BEGINNINGS

OF THERAPY

At no time is one more likely to gather fresh impressions than on first sight. A depressed woman, whom I shall call Mrs. Selma Miller, dark-haired and middle-aged, entered my office staring downward. Once inside, without looking at me first, she glanced quickly around, tossed her head, and declared: "Hmm. No plants in here. No living thing." Then, while I momentarily pondered what sort of person would not have at least one little plant in his office, she sat down and told me about herself. She was struggling to prevent the breakup of her third marriage. She had been an adopted child. Her parents had had natural children after she had entered their lives, but she had never felt on an equal footing. She had been a clinging wife who feared abandonment, and it had happened twice and was about to happen again.

Usually, I like to hear the patient's account of himself or herself with a minimum of questioning and intervention. I'll become active if I must, but the patient's need or reluctance to speak of one area or another is important to observe. A forceful attempt to get the information may elicit facts but not the inner life. The patient, after all, is in the strange, even the absurd situation of revealing private material to a complete stranger. Adequate recognition of this fact will normally add a note of ease. It is good to remember that it is reasonable that the patient choose what will and will not be disclosed at any time. Patients who immediately spill everything out, as if on cue, are showing a failure to guard their best interests, a kind of blind confidence which is still unearned, based usually on extreme pressure to make contact. Toward the end of the hour, I came back to her opening comment, and told her that I thought she had immediately regarded me as a person unlikely to be mothering, as if a preconception were confirmed, even without her having laid eyes on me. This impression of hers had a great deal to do with her search for a really mothering person, and her unhappiness, sometimes even despair, that this had been missing from her life. In fact, I said, it would probably have been more convenient, in a way, to be able to discount me at the very outset, so as not to embark upon a relationship based on hope which she expected to lead to disappointment anyway.

The patient was very interested. I'd shown that I had an ability to observe closely, to remember what she said, and to assign sensible meaning to what would often be discarded as "meaningless" or "casual." The patient was taken seriously. This in itself spoke against her inference that I was not going to be motherly.

My first glimpse of another patient, Mrs. Doris Brown, made me think of an enormous bird. It was something in her posture, her aquiline nose, her alert and darting eyes, her seemingly windblown red hair, which billowed down her back to her waist. And then, once in the office, to which she had immediate antipathy (furniture all wrong, spaces incorrectly arranged, color scheme boring), she repeatedly jumped up from the chair and looked around. She was trying to size me up by sizing up things that stood for me, probably alarmed in some way at my newness and unpredictability, and as she did so she confirmed the birdlike impression, one who moves around suddenly and frequently. Possibly, I thought, what she really wants to do is soar on outspread wings, or perhaps she thinks I might stop her from moving entirely. Mrs. Brown had lived in seven different locations, in the United States and abroad, in the previous ten years. Her henpecked husband was willing to go anywhere. Her son and daughter were unable to focus on schoolwork. She dreamed of a career as a painter, a tranquil and creative life in a wonderful studio, with the strains of chamber music in the background.

Mrs. Brown had a number of semideveloped artistic talents, but had never been able to bring any one of them to maturity. This was an important symptom of a more generalized inability to step forward and live her life. In fact, she frequently imagined methods of putting an end to it.

I was being given a full measure of information immediately, if only I could grasp it. One does require a bit of time to think. One cannot usually say something right away, as with Selma Miller, especially in an initial interview, and it may be days, weeks, or months, before connections form that begin to make sense. Her spate of criticism was similar to Mrs. Miller's remark about my plantless condition. Her movements about the room showed an action orientation, an immediate physical entry into the unsatisfactory environment, and an unwillingness to limit herself to a single vantage point. There was a strange kind of affection in her criticism of my decor, a woman chastising the aesthetically incompetent man who finds such matters of lesser importance than his arduous doctorly work. She intended to throw me off my guard by her spontaneity, to make me lose my staid footing in routine, so that I would see her freshly, not as just another depressed woman consulting an analyst. Her energetic attack on my taste presented her as hardly depressed at all. She would not let herself be seen as a typical case of anything. I would not have a diagnostic victory, not now, and, as it turned out, not later either, not at least without an intricate and relentless process of understanding her fear of standing absolutely still.

Beginnings take place when the telephone rings and your colleague asks you if you have time to see someone, and gives a thumbnail description of who it is and what he knows. The picture forms right away, and you are preoccupied in the odd moment with who this will turn out to be. You get another phone call, from the patient this time, and the voice alone, the style of presentation, fills you with information. Your own reaction will often also say a great deal. For example, I usually try to be businesslike on the phone, with no questions about the nature of the problem. But once in a while I find myself asking one or more, and wondering why. Is this an especially seductive patient, or is this a patient who will not come after all? So many patients don't make it at the start, miss appointments, forget them, get delayed in traffic. I know about the tremendous anxiety they have. I study my own awkwardness for clues about the way the patient is affecting me. Is this a taste of what is to come? Am I reacting to something in the telephone manner, or something I had heard from the referring colleague? Do I feel the person receding from me even on this first contact?

Dennis Carroll, a lawyer, was referred for a phobic condition which started with heights, progressed to knives and then to rooms with closed doors. His life had been getting difficult. On the telephone, I responded to a certain urgency in his voice by asking whether he wanted an appointment immediately and, later, whether he knew where my office was. He had put me off balance.

He presented himself as an impeccably dressed and, at first, arrogant person. He volunteered next to no information, and began with a series of questions about me and my education. I told him something of my background, and then focused on his fear of the unknown element (was I someone to whom he would become phobic?), and his loss of his customary role in professional situations as the authority himself. I did not attempt to make statements about paranoid fear, but only to acknowledge his concern with who I was, and to give him a chance to observe me and my behavior through lengthy discussion. This was a kind of reassurance, my meeting what I regarded as a pressing need.

When he began to speak of himself, Mr. Carroll's arrogance gave way to obvious fear. He had a constricted voice that seemed about to crack. Since his anxiety had nearly paralyzed him, it would have been ill-advised to put any further pressure on him. After the initial bout of awkwardness on the telephone, I was able to initiate a process by which he could let himself become a patient.

Receiving information, evaluating meanings, and providing some combination of support and beginning insight proceed best if the therapist is not striving to attract the patient's interest in continuing with him. It's hard to avoid this attitude if you are in need of patients or require success each time. Rejection is hard to bear at any time, but no more so than at the beginning of a career. When it is one's very personality that is the instrument of treatment, professional rejection trenches upon personal rejection. The effort to present oneself in a good light may bring forth a high level of function, assuming the anxiety level isn't *too* high, and one must know that indifference is hardly the attitude a patient is likely to want in a therapist. One is, at the outset, demonstrating something of the process into which the patient may wish to enter more fully. My behavior with Dennis Carroll is an example of recognizing the difficulty a person may have in letting himself be a patient. Such a person need not encounter an overflowing warmth, nor should he have to put up with total blankness. What he wants to find is a therapist whose behavior implies a capacity to listen carefully and make intelligent judgments.

Under the sway of learning to do psychotherapy, the beginner may think that he should be able to appeal to every patient who comes his way, and it is a fact that the longer he practices, the more he *will* be able to behave in a way that meets the patient's immediate needs and increases the likelihood that the patient will want to continue (if that is indicated). But no matter how long he practices, he will find that some patients will decide against him. A woman who had had several years of therapy with female therapists came to me on referral, but was consulting a woman therapist concurrently. She vacillated between us, telling me that her instinct was to see me, though she was tempted to resume with a woman. Her father, a well-known figure in the motion picture industry, had been quite rejecting in her adolescence, and overly attentive to the changes in her body. She was embarrassed by his calling attention to her when his friends were visiting.

As she made her comparison of therapists, she probably indulged an appetite for stimulating competition between parent surrogates. And then, frightened of coming face to face with a revival of the relationship to her father, she chose to see a woman once more. Or perhaps she found the other therapist's approach a better one for other reasons.

Sometimes the chemistry is wrong. The communication may not get off the ground at the start, for reasons that may have nothing to do with the ultimate "fit" of patient and therapist. A dentist consulted me at a time when I was in great distress. I had difficulty in listening to him, as I waited for the phone to ring. My temporary loss of attentiveness put him off and he did not return. On another occasion, a woman who visited fortunetellers told me how she survived childhood in an orphanage, after her rejecting mother accidentally shot herself. She presented a coherent account of her moving struggle to establish a life of her own, and to form relationships that were mutually enriching. However, at the end of the hour she indicated that a visit to a psychic three weeks earlier had included the warning that she beware of a tall man. This was enough. There was no time to deal with this issue, and I never saw her again.

15.

THE

TRANSFERENCE

Psychotherapy may be confined to a single hour or stretch into years of a several-times-per-week schedule of sessions. It may feature an active, inquiring approach, or a quiet one with a good deal of silence. It may sound to an outsider something like an ordinary conversation, with so much give-and-take that it would seem that the therapist is showing no restraint at all. But to know what is going on, one would have to know what was in his mind.

Understanding the transference reveals the deepest secrets. Transference occurs when the therapist is experienced as if he were one or more important figures in the childhood of the patient. Recognition of this phenomenon may be gained through observation, reflection, and supervision, in the absence of one's own therapy, but in that case is likely to be limited.

Knowledge of the transference forms an essential part of the framework within which therapy can unfold, the unspoken source of the therapist's poise. It imparts an underlying strength to his remarks. Aside from what he may have received in a personal way from his own treatment, the single biggest benefit to his work as a therapist will have been convincing contact with transference. This is accompanied by the realization that no matter what the differences between patient and therapist, the shared qualities build a vital bridge between them.

Knowledge of the transference is earned through repeated experiences of recognizing in his own therapist's interpretations an unparalleled grasp of his state of mind, instantly recognizable as correct, and yet, just before, unconscious. He becomes acutely aware of the ways in which he uses the figure of his analyst to reproduce the unfinished conflicts of his childhood. The therapist knows that the past colors all relating, but, like sunlight, requires special study before its complex nature can be appreciated. Once it has become second nature to take note of transference phenomena, the practitioner's struggle to perceive them will be easier. He can then observe the entire field before him with the "evenly suspended attention" that Freud recommended, and can often say a great deal without worry that it will interfere with the emergence of the transference. This awareness of the importance of the medium of the past through which the present is perceived enables the analyst to correct and revise his impressions, in the effort to arrive at an improved approximation of "reality."

Second in importance only to transference is the phenomenon known as resistance. The patient experiences conflict when rejected unconscious ideas threaten to become conscious. He closes up, the hour becomes impoverished, the free flow of thought is interrupted. The therapist then pays special attention to defenses, and hopes to discern what the patient fears and how he defends himself against it. This may take several hours, or only a few minutes, depending on the stage of treatment and the extent of the patient's anxiety. Therapy always occurs in a fashion in which openness alternates with resistance. Every step forward is inevitably followed by a tendency to stop or to regress. Desires move toward expression until conflict halts the train of associations that would result in their emergence into consciousness.

This can be discouraging to the patient, and to the beginning therapist, but after a while the therapist comes to expect it, and not to be thrown off balance.

If therapy is going to result from the initial interviews, then it begins immediately. Inasmuch as everything that takes place between therapist and patient is part of the therapy relationship, the introductory contacts must be regarded as influences. Yet, in the very first diagnostic interviews, the therapist may be in a slightly less disciplined mood. He may permit a spontaneous comment here and there—a remark on the weather, an acknowledgment of familiarity with a location—because he wishes to make the patient comfortable, or because he knows that a more strictly anonymous role is likely to be ahead, and, as in the very last stages, when he reemerges from a long exile, he demonstrates that he is only a human being after all. Whatever the therapist chooses to do, the process of therapy will have been set in motion the moment the prospective patient has made contact.

Free association plays an indispensable part in mobilizing the forces that will permit a transference to develop. Some patients will naturally ask what they should do to participate effectively, and a simple statement to the effect that they should attempt to say everything they are thinking, no matter how irrelevant, trivial, or embarrassing, can then be made. Ordinarily, it has little meaning at the beginning, even if understood. Patients can't believe that this really helps. They continue to think that selection of material for discussion is indispensable to efficient treatment. This is especially so when treatment is once or twice a week. Naturally, they do not want to waste time and tend to approach the work by searching actively for what is relevant. And this is acceptable for the time being. They are protecting themselves from experiences of the irrational, which seem to them hindrances to a practical outcome. They cannot bear to consider the arduous detour that attention to transference entails, preferring instead to apply "common sense" to achieve what they are after more swiftly.

The therapist may open up the subject of resistance by calling the patient's attention to the avoidance of free association. To a considerable extent, learning to use free association is a product of paying ever-increasing attention to one's thought process, and this is demonstrated first by the accuracy of the therapist's comments. The patient observes how the *therapist* has observed, reflected, processed, connected, and, finally, articulated an idea that is based on information from the patient, and how he has been able to wait until the relevant pieces of information have been given. This motivates the patient to look at himself more and more carefully, in search of those thoughts that will give him access to the deeper reaches of his emotional life, and to report these thoughts to the therapist. Once this has taken root, free association will assume meaning.

The first effective interpretation of transference, which is often a major turning point for a patient, usually produces a confused combination of optimism, awe, and discouragement, and leads to further manifestations of transference, quickly followed by resistance. The earth opens and there, for a brief moment, lies the illuminated unconscious, a succession of receding worlds, nameless and awful. Knowledge of this terrain becomes immediately indispensable, for, however strange, it is seen to be part of one's own self.

Early in analysis, hearing that I would be away for a week, a patient asked me where I was planning to go. She was alarmed that she would not know how to reach me if she needed to talk to me. I had explained that another doctor would be available for emergencies, or, if need be, that I could be reached through my telephone exchange. This seemed to make no difference to her. She wanted to know exactly where I would be, primarily, I thought, to enable her to imagine me in the correct setting, a way of retaining my presence through an image. When I told her as much, she felt belittled. I said it sounded as if she were reexperiencing with me the kind of thing that happened in childhood with her father, from whom she had yearned for understanding and affection, and, in the version of this relationship presented at the start of her therapy, got very little. At this, she fell into tears, which went on until the hour was over. Weeks passed, in which she reported herself morose and despairing all day long, for no apparent reason. In the meantime, she stopped telling me anything other than the most prosaic and uncharged facts about her life, and occasional anecdotes about her activities as a social worker. When I greeted her in the waiting room, she would stare at me intently, as if frightened and unable to make a judgment about who or what I was. Attention to her fear of revealing more of herself than felt comfortable, more of herself than she could, in a sense, *control,* since she couldn't control my thought process, gradually led to a resumption of communication, during which she became enthusiastic. Small insights excited her and she enjoyed telling me dreams. The focus shifted to the past, and away from the here and now, but eventually her fear of the chance that I might reject her saturated the atmosphere once again.

It would seem that what I said should have provided relief, and over the course of time, by giving her a perspective from which to reevaluate her experience, it did. But in the short run, it sounded like a confirmation of her worst fears. It was part of the seeming reenactment of old struggles and old pain, in precisely the environment that was intended to help her overcome the distortions in her development that had been their result. The very fact that she did suffer in the wake of my comparison of her relationship to me and that to her father made her infer that I *intended* to hurt her. Only when she could consider the possibility that pain experienced in analysis might not be an intended result of interpretations could she begin to differentiate her father, a refugee from Hungary, from myself. For the time being, she felt trapped with a fanatically cold father, and there were even moments when she thought I was speaking with an accent like his. She was awed by the insight, discouraged by the link made between present and past, and by the feeling that whatever she did, she couldn't escape the past. Yet she was also hopeful that here was a process that could give her access to what had been hidden away for so long. She was disturbed that it took another person to relay the necessary insight, that she did not possess the ability to provide for her own needs. This seemed to mean a long process of dependency. In a sense, the working out of all these themes constituted the totality of the treatment.

Another patient, a talented interior designer in her thirties named Vivian Andrews, squinted at me through her thick lenses at the beginning of every hour. She confirmed that she was trying to decide what sort of mood I was in. She had always considered herself something of a bother to people, partly because of congenitally poor vision, but especially because of a chronic depression, which she kept hidden as much as possible. After her father's untimely death when she was seven years old, for which she secretly blamed her demands for love from him, she had become a model child. People were amazed at how little evidence there was of that devastating loss. The more she had presented herself as the precocious master of tragedy, the less attention they paid to her invisible sorrow. She had suppressed it all, but not without superficializing her relationships. She had to delete the emotional dimension because, inevitably, it led down to her sadness, her outrage, and her helplessness. In the expression of emotion that had been set loose by her therapy, she naturally feared a reenactment of her traumatic loss. When I said so, there was a moment of silence. She acted slightly stunned and disbelieving, and then resumed, with a babble of remembrances from early days, at first excited, almost joyful, but quickly accompanied by tears. The flow of her associations improved, but then for hours she became inaccessible, and continued to examine me for clues to my moods. The more of her inner life I could be expected to "bear," the more she might be expected to reveal, though erratically, with one crisis after another, as she fought off the dark emotions to which she had sworn never to give way.

It happened that after a while—this is so often the case —merely being in my office was enough to bring forth tears, for she observed me looking at her with eyes that saw through to the pain, and didn't have her customary defense against either knowing about it herself or showing it to others. But instead of concentrating only on a series of interpretations about her situation, I responded to her questions, reaffirming all the while that I knew more and more about the dimensions of the burden she had been carrying, and particularly that she had done without the comfort that she had needed as a child, and needed right now, just as if she were a child still. When she wanted to consult a gynecologist, I recommended one to her. When she talked about something wrong with her car, I happened to know what the problem was and told her. It was, in short, a very supportive therapy, and there was no difficulty mixing it with recurrent attention to the transference. She could not have sustained herself in depriving conditions without this more direct support, and she gained strength to face the transference through my availability in other ways. The amount of silence she could tolerate from me was limited, though it increased over time.

The evident principle is that you don't ask more of a patient than she is capable of giving. You must begin to make your judgments in this regard right at the beginning. You don't ask a schizophrenic to lie down and free associate, since the patient is already tormented by his uncontrolled thoughts, night and day. That patient needs to be pulled together with a very active effort to make sense. And one doesn't ask of any fragile and frightened patient, psychotic or not, that he or she bear long periods of being stared at before you offer a statement. It is this sort of thing that earns psychotherapists a bad name. There is a thin line separating the fruitless imposition of silence, a sort of peacock preening of the disciplined and otherworldly therapist, and the indispensable period of silent reflection, in which the patient is given room to express himself, including his articulations of transference, and the therapist is given room to think about what he has been hearing. The therapist needs to be silent sometimes. He may warn the patient that this will be so. Descriptions of the flow of therapy and the necessity for silences carry the message that the process is a rational one, that some form of magic is not being practiced. The reasonableness of psychotherapy makes it something that the patient may in time apply to himself, and not the sole province of the therapist.

Explanations of the nature of transference can be part of the orientation process as well, in those moments when it is not saturating the relationship. If the patient asks me how the therapy works, I am not averse to explaining it this way: "When you come to see someone regularly, tell him a great deal about your life, and know next to nothing about his, a strange kind of relationship begins to form. You start to have feelings about the other person which, because you know so little about him, are likely to tell a great deal about yourself. Usually, he will remind you of one or more people from the earlier part of your life, and as you feel that more and more, you are in a position to look at those old relationships as if they were in the present time. Forgotten experiences come back and you can rethink your life in the light of what you learned later on, but had never applied to formative times.

Old conflicts that left a mark on you can now be rethought. And the point of all this is not to become obsessed with the past but to put it behind you. So much of it might have been forcibly forgotten, because of being too painful and seemingly useless to think and feel about. But that didn't mean that it stopped influencing you. On the contrary, whatever conflicts are undigested and unsorted out and unresolved probably continue to influence your life in profound ways. With this method, there is a chance of understanding it well enough to forget it and live your life more fully in the present."

Such explanations do not foreclose a deep and spontaneous experience in therapy. On the contrary, they seem to provide the support necessary for many patients to take the required chances. Such summaries can be profitably repeated later on, as the therapist helps the patient stand away from total immersion and look at what is taking place. By providing an overview, they afford the patient a sense of relief and support for the courage it takes to permit himself to include another person in the process of finding out those things about himself that he never wanted to know. Yet it is done without coaxing, only by providing relevant information.

However, in emergency situations, there may be none of the atmosphere of equanimity, and something else is called for. Active intervention may be indispensable. A patient came to me in panic over the unexpected death of her daughter. She was agitated, could not sit in the chair, paced back and forth wringing her hands and repeating: "What will I do, she's dead, she's dead, what will I do, oh, God." No process of slow unfolding was about to occur. She was drowning in panic and needed relief.

Though acutely aware of this, I felt at first that, since I knew nothing about her, I had nothing to offer. No clever and arresting interpretation was going to nullify the fact that her daughter was dead, and for the moment, my presence was simply not enough. That was her message: nothing is enough. She projected her helplessness frantically, as a kind of contagion. I began to ask her questions about herself and her daughter, in order to form a picture of their relationship, interspersing comments that showed that I was actively making connections as she spoke, not leaving gaps in the interchange (no dead silence to remind her of death itself). I was trying to provide a context for the scattering of thoughts that assailed her. This was necessary several times a week for about a month, after which there was a relaxation of anxiety. During that time, it became clear that the death of her sister before her birth had caused her to feel guilt throughout her childhood (as if she had displaced her), which was reactivated by the overwhelming grief and loss when her daughter died. There had also been a subtly competitive relationship to her daughter, whose musical talent far overshadowed the more rudimentary skills of my patient, who had always wanted to be a concert pianist. When, finally, she dreamed of her daughter, could actually see her as a moving, apparently living person, she was immensely reassured. This hallucinatory recovery of one whom she believed she would never see again provided that necessary bit of support for a calmer and more extended exploration of the elements of her anxiety, which ended a few months later with a resumption of functioning. Her grief, of course, continued.

Suicidal emergencies also call for a more active role. Suicide is a possibility at almost any stage in therapy with certain patients, and is approached differently in each case. In the acute situation, a rapid evaluation must be made to determine how to prevent it. There are those professionals who believe that a patient has the right to take his own life, and should not be stopped. One may accept this belief under certain circumstances, such as in the face of a terminal disease. I find it irresponsible to invoke it when faced with anything less, especially where the possibility is distinct. There are situations that require forceful restraint, others that will respond to drugs, and others that require psychotherapy. Combinations of these are frequently necessary. The provision of support may take many forms. A patient may be in a panic because he cannot control his suicidal urge, and needs someone who can stop him from acting on it. The immediate threat demands attention. Once it has abated, longer-term therapy may be undertaken.

A young writer, rejected by his girlfriend, came to me after having slit his wrists. He was glad to have been discovered by a friend before it was too late, but continued to be acutely disturbed by the emotions of loss and rejection. Coming to my office every day, including weekends, for a period of two weeks, gave him an outlet for his panic and the beginning of a means of expressing it in the context of a relationship. After the initial phase, he was able to make good use of a twice-weekly schedule for some months. In the calmer, more extended evaluation of the underlying problem, it seemed advisable that he undertake an analysis. My rescuer role stimulated a tendency to view me as the older cousin of childhood who had counseled him during periods when his mother's alcoholic bouts left him without protection from a brutal father. A homosexual transference supervened, revealing the source of his panic to have been the fear that the loss of his girlfriend would push him toward a man for sexual satisfaction, a way of staving off despair. His initial, extraordinary series of hours, seven days a week, had provided a sense of a safe haven in which to begin to look carefully at unconscious urges to which words had never been given.

Experience is indispensable when one is faced with such an acute situation. Having thought his way through countless problems in the reconstruction of reality from clues given in the consultation room, the therapist has at his disposal a stock of possibilities with which to calm *himself* in the face of a threat from the patient. This is the fruit of his own analysis as well as of all the crisis situations with which he has had to cope, going all the way back to medical school. He knows that there are times when patients need a real and present person. He faces the patient's welter of emotions squarely, without taking refuge in a line of interpretation that requires more presence of mind than the patient possesses at the moment. He holds firm, without prescribing drugs to blot out his own powerlessness, or letting himself get angry at the patient for not responding in a way that vindicates the value of his remarks, or insisting on any particular set of ideas. This steadiness is a prerequisite for collecting the required information with which to gain understanding. He finds his way to a sense of adequacy slowly.

In the case of the panic-stricken patients I have described, any steady hand and inquiring mind would have been of immediate use, but beyond the initial period, when calming was the main task, only a point of view that could connect past and present on target could provide the required basis for a permanent change.

16.

TIME, MONEY,

AND

CONFIDENTIALITY

Part of the process by which a course of psychotherapy is initiated consists of practical arrangements of time and money. Fee ranges are the arbitrary results of market forces, though a therapist's need for and attitude toward money also determine what he asks for his services. The amount of the fee may bear little relation to the quality of the work.

In this work you have only your conscience to answer to. Any element of exploitation compromises your ability to function. Regarding the patient as someone to use is obviously antithetical to a helping attitude. Becoming aware that a fee is excessive may prompt the therapist to look into himself for the meaning the patient has to him.

On the other hand, some therapists have difficulty in asking enough for their services, or in insisting that it be paid in a timely fashion. Not to take a firm stand in this area is to invite depreciation of one's efforts. It is unlikely that patients in such a situation will regard the therapist's work with sufficient respect to make good use of it.

Like any other element in the interaction with a patient, the therapist's attitude toward the fee expresses something. The progress of one's comfort with the work can be measured by the extent to which the fee becomes less and less a subject of conflict. One begins to feel that a certain amount of compensation is simply deserved. Some therapists set aside time for patients who can afford less than the average fee, or give of themselves without compensation as teachers or supervisors at clinics, part of an honored tradition in the helping professions. Some judge that they deserve higher-than-average fees, based on an opinion of their abilities that may or may not be well founded. Others are more flexible. The matter does not rest with the setting of a fee, however, for every time a bill is payable the matter of the fee can reintrude itself and become a vehicle for understanding the patient. A therapist who has not come to terms with money in his own life will find it difficult to utilize the opportunity for understanding provided by the way money is handled by the patient.

A patient who was doing well in once-weekly therapy was chronically late in paying his bill. He was a man of quite considerable wealth, but this wealth was "tied up" in stocks, and he gave the appearance of struggling month to month to meet his obligations. Not only did he delay payment for weeks, but he didn't even mention it or ask whether I agreed to it. In dire need of understanding the fear of intimacy which had marked him since childhood, he consistently exploited others in daily life. I had called his attention to the avoidance of money issues a number of times, but he continued to play out his pattern of delay. Finally, I insisted that he recognize that his behavior had meaning. He was depreciating me by assuming that I could simply wait, which was also a form of tacit borrowing, and at the same time he was turning me into a "nice guy" by proceeding in an atmosphere in which his failure to pay his bill on time was not a central topic. In other words, he was making it easier for himself by including a habitual element of exploitation. It was as if he were stealing what he received, on the assumption that it would not have been freely given. In essence, he feared me as a fully effective person, and required some means by which he could make me less so. The patient was interested in all this, but saddened, and presented himself as the injured innocent, a person who meant well but was being misunderstood. He sent his checks in the mail, avoiding whatever emotions would have accompanied direct payment.

Later exploration showed that he regarded payment as a contaminant of treatment, something that undermined my credibility as a genuinely interested person. He thought I deserved to be paid but would have liked to pay me nothing. In that way, he could be sure I was seeing him because I wanted to, not "because of" the money. Making me wait gave him some yield in this area. Yes, he could feel better about someone who would be willing to brook delay. And he could sweeten his experience by "getting away" with something.

This patient, an investment banker whose every working moment was concerned with money, was skilled at evoking defensiveness in that area. He required consistent frankness, if he was ever going to be able to look carefully at what people expect of each other and what they deserve. He found it difficult to understand the nature of a close tie to another person, because he feared that in such a situation a lifelong devotion to the accumulation of wealth would be reversed, that he would be depleted of all resources and independence. He thought in financial terms, but what bothered him was the unmeasurable world, the world of emotion. He knew he would begin to feel dependent, with everything of value regarded as in the province of the one on whom he depended—the therapist, in this instance. In such circumstances, he would regress to primal times, when an infant's need for his mother would rule his life again, all development snatched away.

Eventually, the therapist comes to know that the fee does not actually pay for the therapy, only for the time set aside in which the therapy is to occur. The fee is an arbitrary, socially determined means by which time is given value. The work itself is literally priceless. No fee covers the work of making someone's life livable or fulfilling. No one can buy another person's sustained and careful attention and the long-term buildup of knowledge that is the necessary basis for insight. This is given voluntarily. True to some extent of most professional work, it is more true of work that entails the use of one's own emotional life for the benefit of someone else. The mastered techniques of the attorney require less of his emotion than the work of the psychoanalyst, or, for that matter, the work of the actor or the sculptor.

Some patients can benefit from as little as one session per week. For psychotherapy, any less is usually impracticable, the rare exception notwithstanding, unless no schedule at all is adopted and the patient is seen as needed. Such courses of treatment can be quite productive, motivated throughout by recurring expressions of interest and need. Five sessions a week are sometimes needed, and not necessarily by analytic patients on the couch. Some, such as the aforementioned writer in homosexual panic, are under such duress that any less, for a while, will not provide the necessary support. All other frequencies are chosen on the basis of the requirements of both patient and therapist. For example, the patient may be able to afford to pay for only one or two sessions a week, while the therapist believes that three would be optimal. A lower fee makes more sessions a possibility, but the therapist must be sure that in accepting less per session, he does not then succumb to a heightened need for evidence that the patient appreciates his generosity.

The "hours" are now forty-five or fifty minutes long as a rule, although there is the occasional variation, from a half hour to an hour and a half. These are arbitrary times which conveniently fit a schedule, but they also appear to be sufficient to allow a substantial unfolding to occur, and there is something useful about regularity and predictability. The regularity of the hour is part of the ground against which the figure of the patient's life appears. It goes with the fee, the office arrangement, and the reliable behavior of the thera- pist. Adherence to arbitrary beginnings and endings calls forth an attitude of discipline from both participants, and requires the patient to face moments of separation that are the result of nothing but the clock. These moments act as stimuli to fantasy about separation and are indispensable for approaching that ramifying subject. Struggles to be on time can be notable for what they reveal about the relationship. Some patients are always a little late, so as not to be in the position of waiting. If the therapist himself is late, they can be seen visibly struggling with volcanic anger, as they try to cope with the humiliation. At the end of the hour, some patients become awkward and forgetful, as a developing order collapses in the emotion of rejection. A comforting closeness falls to bits in the coldness of ending. Much of this would be unavailable in the hypothetical situation of vari- able hours, suited to apparent need. Ultimately, the hour's length becomes something sturdy, to be relied upon in the struggle for self-knowledge. It represents the world of unyielding reality, the rock upon which all development must be founded.

The frequency is determined not only by what is re- quired for progress or what the patient can afford. It is affected also by the patient's requirements for distance or closeness. The patient who delayed payment should have been seeing me four times a week at that stage of treatment, but would agree to two sessions only. Again, he said this had to do with money. But in fact it represented his fear of closeness, which I respected, knowing that eventually we would have to address it, and to the extent that it was under- stood, he would relax his defense and come to see me more often. Some patients may find a break of any kind so stressful to contemplate that they would gladly come seven times a week if possible. Unable to feel complete without daily contact with the therapist, they demonstrate a failure to bear separateness which is traceable to the early years, or, sometimes, a struggle with hostile wishes that generate fantasies about the therapist, against which evidence of his survival is a necessary reassurance. All patients will sooner or later manifest reactions to separation, as progress in therapy makes for a kind of symbiotic closeness, with roots that reach deep. If patients are coming only twice a week, I prefer to see them on successive days, precisely to make a setting for the emergence of feelings of loss, if such feelings are pressing for expression.

Ordinarily, practical considerations determine which hours a patient comes. It is a matter of taking two schedules into account. But sometimes, the nature of the patient's problem plays a role. Patients who evoke sleepiness or boredom are best not seen in the early afternoon. The effort to be alert must be redoubled by fluctuations in blood sugar after lunch. I would rather see them sometime during the morning. And if it is possible to see a patient at the same hour each day, this enhances the sense of regularity, the ground of treatment.

Insurance forms have forced their way into our profession and compromised the absolute nature of confidentiality. They must be prepared if patients are to receive compensation. But care is required. I strictly limit what I am willing to disclose to dates of treatment, fee, diagnosis, and my name, address, taxpayer number, telephone number. The diagnosis rendered is the least dire one consistent with truth. Nothing that is disclosed by a patient to a therapist is anyone else's business, and this is a fundamental part of a therapeutic environment. It is all too easy to become accustomed to intrusions, but every single accommodation, no matter how socially or economically rationalized, detracts from the vitality of the therapy. As a therapist in training, one may view therapy through a one-way mirror, see patients interviewed before audiences large and small, and present tape recordings to one's supervisors. It is part of the way a clinic runs, and the patients are compensated for this sharing of information by a heightened degree of expertise and a lower fee. Yet this, too, takes a toll. University hospitals that put the teaching value of a case above all other considerations are implementing a policy that transgresses the more fundamental one of the helping professions: rendering aid where it is needed. Wherever this spirit is compromised, the integrity of the therapist is compromised, in the direction of self-centeredness rather than service.

It need not be emphasized that therapists are not selfless. They are interested in their own growth as people, in their education, professional standing, and prosperity. But it is their special pride that they are preoccupied with positioning themselves vis-à-vis patients in such a way that they can *give,* and in the service of that goal they take up attitudes that are intended to safeguard the required environment. The intrusions of others on these positions can become a serious problem.

A twenty-two-year-old man became suicidal and his uncle packed up his drug supply and sent it to my office by messenger. He was acting on his nephew's behalf, but I regarded this gesture as an intrusion. I would address my patient's feelings, without my acting as custodian of his drugs. I sent the package back without comment.

A patient's father telephoned and left a message for unknown reasons. I told the patient about it the next day. It was left that she would decide what to do about it. This may seem a bit rude, but there is no reason for the therapist to be merely responsive to whatever impulse a relative may have.

A patient referred a friend to me, and then asked if she had come in. I told her that it didn't seem fitting to answer, that whatever occurred or not between her friend and me couldn't be discussed with anyone. She would receive the same kind of confidentiality.

A gynecologist referred several people to me. On a social occasion, he asked me how they were doing. "Good," I said, feeling hesitant to say even this much, while tempted to say even more. How easy it would have been to mention this or that detail, but he quickly realized that I was going to be closemouthed, smiled at me, and went on to another subject.

Cooperation with other professionals in the patient's life may be desirable or even necessary. The patient must know and approve of the communication, however, and this usually puts limits on what can be discussed. Much depends on the discretion of both parties. A former patient who learned she was dying authorized me to communicate with her oncologist. A conversation on the advisability of disclosing to the patient how much time she had left was not revealed to the patient. I judged that she should not have to be bothered with such matters as our conversation. I told the oncologist that she needed some measure of hope with which to cope with the unstoppable reality that was pressing in on her, that he should continue to talk about the potential outcomes of chemotherapy, while trying all relevant drugs. I believe he knew all this anyway. I was just confirming my agreement with it.

One day she came in with a wig to conceal the total baldness that was a side effect of chemotherapy. After a period in which it seemed she was going to elude this painful blow to her already battered self-esteem, it had caught up with her anyway. She smiled and chatted away, putting on a front, as if I were the one who required support for hope, as if I should not feel let down, and as if she could handle anything. Her ability to deny was working overtime, making of her remaining days something more than mere abject misery. I asked myself whether I had attracted this concern by showing signs of the struggle to find a point of view that offered what I thought she needed. I had been wary of the influence of experiences of loss in my own life on the work of helping my patient, and thought I had succeeded in remaining focused on her and her alone. But in what turned out to be the final hour of our work, processes of projection and introjection had rendered us something of a mother/infant couple, each the counterpart of the other. To an outsider, it would have seemed just another hour in which a therapist was trying to help a patient. Nothing dramatic was visible. But I was stricken by the inevitability of this fine young woman's early death. I listened to her remarks about chemotherapy with interest and with a sense of denial. In a way, I had kept her dying away from me and now a kind of mutual aid was joining us together. She had asked that I call her by her first name when she came back to me with her fatal illness. The strict procedures of the earlier, successful therapy were now inappropriate. She needed a more visibly human presence, yet not one who discarded order, not one who deprived her of a reliable arena in which to get her bearings. As she stood up to leave, with obvious effort, I said, thinking it was true: "I'll see you next week, Lisa."

The ways of integrity are not simple.

17.

THE MIDDLE PHASE
OF THERAPY

The more time therapist and patient spend together, the greater the likelihood that a blurring of perceptions will occur. The freshness of first impressions and insights gives way to the flatness of more familiar ones. This is naturally more exaggerated in the patient, who is denied more than minimal knowledge of the therapist, but it is true to some extent for the therapist as well. Partly to overcome this mutual mood, therapists will often attempt to clarify the nature of the relationship. By invoking the therapeutic process the therapist thereby redefines the two principal characters, both separating them in order to understand the lapsed interaction, and at the same time extricating himself from the flattening effect of long periods together. He regains a sense of restraint, an ability to feel "held" by the abilities resulting from his education and experience. In turn, this refound poise makes it possible for him to "hold" the patient in an unfolding process. It makes it possible to *hear* the patient anew as well, instead of losing acuity for nuance and novelty.

Concerning this crucial issue of examining the process for themselves, psychoanalysts almost always pose the question: "But is it really psychoanalysis?" by which they attempt to measure a given piece of work against a standard they have in mind. This effort helps them to persist in inevitably

lengthy and difficult treatments. To disregard such a judgment is to wander in the wilderness, subject to pragmatic
impulses to make the patient feel better, rather than being
able to maintain the continuity of the treatment.

Part of the struggle also involves keeping psychoanalysis
developing as a modality of treatment and as a general psychology, and not only practicing psychoanalysis for the patient at hand. On this grander scale, it includes matters of
hope for mankind, which gains substantially from a body of
knowledge that accurately systematizes the chaos of human
emotional experience.

There's a long history to attempts to hold on to a defini-
tion of psychoanalysis, beginning with Freud, whose own
perspective shifted radically at times. His most famous
change was the 1897 renunciation of the theory that his
neurotic patients had all been seduced in childhood. After
that, his attention turned to the world of fantasy as a force
in human emotional life. Jung, Adler, Rank, Stekel, Reich,
and others were expelled from the movement for advocat-
ing theories that clashed with Freud's. In his time, he was the
sole arbiter of what deserved the name of psychoanalysis.
After his death, a proliferation of viewpoints competed for
attention, and they continue to do so.

A few basic ideas unite all analysts, however. Foremost
among them is that the understanding of the transference is
the backbone of the work. Generally speaking, an intense
schedule of sessions of uniform length, with the analyst
behaving anonymously, are essential elements in the setting
that makes the development and understanding of transference possible. Free association gives the analyst access to
what he needs to know, both through what is expressed in
the associations and through the incidents of resistance
when the process is interrupted. These few ideas provide
criteria by which a given analyst may judge how well he is
adhering to the basics. There are times, of course, when
circumstances may require variation. But he strives to clarify

those instances, to understand precisely why he does deviate, and to return to a more classical stance when he can. He regards himself as a scientist who is pursuing a method that allows the truth to come to light, and in this pursuit he wants to avoid whatever influence he might tend to have on the nature of what emerges. He wants to be able to rely on its independence from his own biases, which entails a fundamental capacity to maintain the separateness of the observed from the observer. The task demands a scrupulous and relentless self-searching, which can never be absolutely pure. Analysts consider their method and the theories of psychology which are associated with that method as high achievements of man, worthy of protection, nurturance, and continuous enlargement. They believe that their constant contact with the real world of human struggle gives them a special rootedness in life as lived, in contrast to those psychologists who derive ideas from experiments or from external behavior alone. They are torn between devotion to a pragmatic end, the relief of suffering, and devotion to an impersonal end, the discovery of data about the way people function. Presumably, finding the truth about a patient is therapeutic in itself. Yet the motivation to help naturally tends to undermine the discipline required for the scientist's pursuit of discovery. And in fact, there are many moments when helping is, in the short run, antithetical to discovering, when, for example, the patient's defenses are reinforced by the analyst's therapeutic behavior. A note of reassurance in the therapist's remarks may reduce the patient's awareness of conflict for the time being. His hope is that, in the long run, lapses in strict technique will make way for deeper revelations from a patient who is increasingly secure in trusting the good intentions and good judgment of his analyst.

The middle phase of psychotherapy has been compared to the middle game in chess, which cannot be taught with clarity the way the opening and closing games can. It is the time when newness has passed, and struggles with conflict and defense take the center of the stage. And in that time, a judgment is eventually made about what outcome is practical and possible and what is not.

The therapist's range of experience is naturally as vast as the range of patients he sees, all the way from the satisfying instance where the pairing of patient and therapist leads to rapid unfolding of conflict and resolution, to the frustrating and slow encounter with rigid patients who have deeply ingrained characterological problems that can change only slightly.

A patient who had had a long analysis many years before came to see me for an outburst of anxiety caused by his discovery that his wife had been having an affair. He was forty-five years old, a black-bearded professor of English, quiet, shy, and now bewildered. He did not wish to see his previous analyst, with whom he was on extremely formal ground. He preferred a more relaxed situation, with a new person. He described his supposedly good marriage, his children, and the shock of finding a letter that disclosed her affair. It had been her only one, as far as he knew, short-lived, over now—but shattering. He had always counted on his excellent marriage as the basis of his sense of security. His parents had been divorced when he was six, and prior to that time he had been mistreated by his mother, who frequently said she wished he were dead. His father was a remote figure, and the child had spent a good deal of time in the streets, with friends, unsupervised, and been taken in by various neighbors, who supplied some of the affection he couldn't get at home.

An older sister had occasionally filled in for his absent mother, but she was unpredictable, sometimes warm and loving, sometimes distant and cool. In the second hour he told me a dream about his wife, in which she appeared in the form of a mother lizard caring for a baby. Tongue darting out to lick the baby in what passed for motherly behavior, she finally bit the baby's neck until blood came forth. He awoke in fear. Lizards are cold-blooded, he said, their body temperature changes with the outside one. They change like his sister changed, and the mothering lizard could not be counted on to remain that way. He felt quite fearful when telling me the dream, and I could immediately connect the dream to his present circumstances, with mother and sister being likened to his wife. He was afraid of the loss of his wife's loving attitude and of his own anticipated demise, the weakening of the bond being evident in her having had the affair. It wasn't merely the real loss of his wife's affection that he feared, but the associated revival of childhood concerns about losing mother's and sister's warmth, which he had required then for his very survival.

This discussion, which he could grasp immediately because of prior treatment, resulted in a decline in anxiety. He became more obviously depressed. His sadness and anger, more fitting responses to his wife's affair, drove him into discussions with her about what had caused her to act as she had. He chose to see me for a total of five interviews, which limited the opportunity for a regressed transference relationship. In the remaining sessions, there were further insights, with the patient feeling that I was supplying him with a steady warmth of interest that had been uncertain in childhood and was now vital. It was a kind of splinting of a fractured life, brief, serviceable, limited. His own healing powers, born in part of prior therapy, could take over and do the necessary work.

Here the middle phase was ushered in by the dream, and permitted a limited therapy to succeed. There were essentially no defenses to deal with, largely because of his prior therapy and our rapid rapport. I did not need to lead the patient through a process of understanding that would make my interpretations meaningful. He could grasp them immediately. Also, the threat of regression was nullified by limiting the number of hours.

A woman in her twenties, Charlotte Bernard, had never been in love. Raised in an atmosphere of quiet desperation between her parents, and deeply devoted to her invalid father, this extremely attractive woman had managed to make herself plain, withdrawn, uninviting, and unavailable. A course of treatment of four months duration resulted, against all expectations, in a highly visible transformation. After the insights relating to her attachment to her father and her unconscious willingness to sacrifice her life for him, she began to select her clothing with care and to respond to the urgings of her friends that she do what she could to make herself more attractive. It was easy. Men began to make overtures. She began to smile. She was fearful and guilt-ridden on occasion, and the work continued to address her fear, but she showed herself capable of making what amounted to a sea change.

Side by side with the idea that change takes work, that defenses require repeated understanding, that every move forward will be followed by some degree of retrenching, and that the ultimate result will always represent a compromise between an ideal vision and the practical limitations of reality—side by side with this sense of limits and difficulty is a totally different one: that change is only an instant away, that the accumulation of a lifetime's suffering may suddenly and decisively be set aside in favor of a new grasp of what life has to offer. One overlooks this principle repeatedly, both as a therapist and as a person, but once it has been seen *in action,* it is, in a sense, unforgettable. It is a kind of ultimate hope, which, activated, can take the therapist confidently into perilous water. Its evangelical undertones may conjure up the subject of religious conversion and be therefore antipathetic to the rational psychotherapist. But the fact that certain people do undergo radical and sudden change, for religious or other reasons, reinforces a belief in the possibility. Such hopefulness may underlie the therapist's efforts in short-term treatment such as I have just described, and make of a brief "middle phase" an exciting and experimental thing.

In contrast to such fortunate situations, in which a process of improvement proceeds smoothly because the patient's flexibility enables the therapist to move effectively, are the more difficult cases, in which the unyielding mechanisms of resistance break down optimism and tax memory for the means of measuring change. For such cases, *the problem of the middle phase is that of keeping hope alive, in both the patient and the therapist.* Hope tends to die in the erosion of perspective typical of such middles. Absorbed in understanding the patient, and embarked on extended explorations possible only where a good deal of time is available, the therapist repeatedly emerges into daylight, naturally seeing his patient anew, or feeling under pressure to do so. What he needs to feel is that he is providing a particular kind of help to someone, as opposed to indulging his appetite for knowledge, enjoying a relationship, or moving at random from one subject to another. Knowing he is conducting a proper form of psychotherapy enables him to tolerate some of the confusion, the blind alleys, the unsatisfactory hours, the fumbling. He must find words that convincingly explain what has been and is taking place. In danger of self-indulgence, in the emotional or intellectual realm, because he is a person before he is a psychotherapist, he must orient himself with up-to-date formulations in order to avoid behavior that represents the pursuit of personal aims. This is a daily matter, a kind of maintenance work. If he withdraws into silence, he asks himself why. If he doesn't understand the nature of the present phase, he asks himself how long he has been confused and what explanation is likely. As his reconsideration of all relevant factors provides him with a new and vital perspective, he regains the necessary hope for continuing the work.

An accountant in analysis for three years grew less and less forthcoming, even as his life situation was greatly improving. He frequently began his hours by saying: "I don't seem to have anything to say," or "Analysis seems so far away now, I didn't want to come here today." I found myself glancing around the office and daydreaming, while he mentioned familiar themes. My unimaginative pages of doodling expressed the stasis well. I had taken only an occasional note and suspected withdrawal in myself whenever I did more than that. In this case, what words I wrote were parts of doodles. The sense of structure began to dissolve. For five or six hours I was unable to orient myself by reviewing recent stages in treatment. Finally, I asked him why he thought he felt as he did about our work. "I don't know," he began. "I know I desperately need your help." I was surprised to hear it, in view of his behavior. "Just as I desperately need Julie" (his estranged wife, with whom he was beginning to reconcile).

I caught a glimmer of his conflict from his use of "desperately," a word that was most untypical of a man who qualified his every judgment, as if tuning a piano. My daydreaming cleared away forthwith.

In the next hour, he told me a dream about a flounder hiding in the mud at the bottom of the ocean, waiting for a predator to pass before he resumed feeding. It was as if he were watching through an aquarium window. He felt nothing. His associations led directly to the analytic situation, and his own hiding from the predator that I was experienced as being. The "feeding" he had been doing in analysis was a secret thing. If he were fully absorbed in the process, he could not be sufficiently aware of danger to him. The improvement in his life meant that he had been receiving something useful from me, this activated a hypervigilant state which was masked by indifference and "floundering." In addition, the aquarium pictorialized the great distance from his own feelings that I could sense in the recent hours. The work now resumed in a lively way.

In the fourth year of the arduous treatment of a patient with severe social anxiety, I found myself losing touch with the process. This excitable man pleaded with me for comment about every new social situation with which he was faced, asking for any kind of support, any hint about what he might do to reduce the level of panic. I had carelessly begun to make statements along the lines he requested. "You've been in this very situation before and it turned out well, didn't it?" I said, glad to hear the immediate relief that came into his voice. "I guess you're right," he said. "I suppose it's foolish of me to get so crazy." On the next such occasion, his pleas were all the greater, and I had to be severe with myself and with him to avoid taking him down a path that might well reduce his restraint in the end and turn his analysis into mere support. He was not a patient with whom one could move easily between different modes of interaction. He required analysis of a strict kind because his defenses were rigidly held and he had the inner strength to benefit from the consequent regression. I identified my own wish for relief from the sense of being the one who deprives, and was able to address the patient's fear of a failure of my ability to give what he needed. This reminded me of the conditions of his childhood, with an ineffectual and depreciated father and an unreliable, emotionally unstable mother. A sense of calm and heightened interest returned to me. The process of differentiating myself from the transference figure he saw me as being gave me access to renewed energy for the work. This fostered the poise my patient needed for the next stage of the work—overcoming the anxiety that was engulfing him.

Selma Miller, the woman who, in her first hour, looked for a plant in my office, proved to be an almost insufferably complaining and boring patient, whom sometimes for weeks on end I dreaded seeing. She had a special way of whining. She would speak in a deteriorated form of English that showed a regression to childlike dependency and loss of form. Then she would lapse into pouting, angry silence and contempt. To her it seemed obvious that I owed so much more than I was delivering. Her persistent attitude led me to examine exactly what I *was* doing. When I was waiting to hear more, trying to digest her communications in order to say something useful and tolerating to my limits the stress of her depreciation, there were times when the whole project seemed unworkable. I would remind myself that she was somehow making me feel as ineffectual as she herself felt, that on occasion I had become more dependent on a favorable response from her than I wanted to admit. I tried to grasp why this was so. And then I saw how her having been an adopted child was connected to the doubts about my ability and wish to give her what she wanted and needed. Having failed to understand the more proximate causes of her mood, I would find logic in the more distant past. With *this* logic in tow, I could make a needed explanatory connection and embark upon a carefully phrased, slowly stated interpretation that would have the effect of shedding the hopelessness in which we had both been dwelling. "Yes, I see that," she would say. "What you mean is . . ." and she would show how she had grasped my insight. This was a recurrent feature of the work with her, and only by bits and pieces of understanding could it be mastered. Insight can easily be forgotten, and remembering and applying it to the many areas of life to which any piece of insight is inevitably relevant takes time and patience. Being an adopted child might seem an unforgettable fact which explained much about her, but her own tendency to forget it tended to make me forget as well, and together we had to retrieve that fact and many others before a solid achievement of understanding her moods and her life could result. Repetition is indispensable and inevitable, and accounts, in part, for the length of a searching treatment.

Vivian Andrews, the woman whose father had died when she was seven, examined me before every hour to see if it was safe to communicate, then unpacked a lifetime of hopelessness, hour after hour. Previously seemingly immune to loss, independent to a fault, she found the therapy situation safe enough to let me see how the opposite had all along been true. I was hard-pressed, even knowing this, to confront the flow of tears in every hour, week after week, and the repeated statement that she couldn't take care of herself, didn't see how she ever would, and didn't think that the therapy was helping, either. How could I sit there and think I was doing her any good, when every ability she once had —to earn a living, to shop, to cook her own food, even make telephone calls to friends—was compromised and practically gone. (In fact, these abilities fluctuated.) My capacity to receive this despair was limited, and I could not have sat still for more than the scheduled fifty minutes. I girded myself for every hour, remembering that she was inducing in me the very state she must have felt her mother was in, after her father had died, a condition of mind characterized by a limited capacity to listen and to respond emotionally. This appreciation for the transference was probably the single most telling ability I had to sustain myself and therefore sustain a continuous line of expression in the patient. She had found a person who could resist being swamped by the emotion that was swamping her.

The mistrust of me that Dennis Carroll, the phobic lawyer, showed in the first hour was to continue through his very long-term therapy. One may think that proper interpretation will dispel suspicion, but in a great many cases, the main work of the therapy is to understand the suspicion. When it has finally abated, the therapy is all but over. The lawyer did, in a sense, become phobic of me, or, more properly, was made so anxious by the possibility of being understood that he filled the hour with intellectualization and exasperating superficialities. Several years passed, in which I tried my best to make sense of what he said, and to return him to the world of emotion by helping him to see what he was actually feeling. They weren't entirely barren years. He would grasp an idea, then have a dream, which caused a certain relief in me, because I could see so many diagnostic elements in it. I would tell him my understanding of it, and he would respond enthusiastically. It was like a grand thaw after a bitter arctic winter. But as soon as he began to unfold, he would grow suspicious again; the fish feeling the barb, he would stop, sometimes in midsentence, go silent, make a trivial comment, and retreat. He was not conscious of the surge of anxiety that must have been interposed between his expressive moments and the inhibited ones. The long work would begin again.

He had come to me a lonely man, an outstanding corporate lawyer with a frustrating marriage and three young children. Alert and intelligent, he had fought his way out of a very depressing childhood into a series of fairly good schools, and then had a chance to practice in a firm notable for its famous clients. Obsessed with detail, he was inward, wary of others. He had found himself undergoing a frightening escalation of phobic experiences, beginning with a longstanding fear of heights, now extreme, and progressing to scissors, and then finally to a claustrophobic terror of rooms with closed doors.

His father had died when he was four and a half. After a few years, his mother had taken Dennis and his older brother to live in France, the country of her birth. There, the brothers were under the care of a housekeeper, while the mother worked. Dennis was independent from an early age, walking the streets of the provincial city by himself, asking someone to buy him a soft drink now and then, sitting alone on the curb for hours on end. His brother spent most of his days and nights at the home of a friend. The patient harbored a lifetime of resentment for his obviously neurotic and ungiving mother and her series of boyfriends, and it was one of the unresolved problems of the treatment that he could not liberate himself from the grip of this fury. In time, it bored me to hear him dwell upon the unsatisfactory encounters with her, but the thing that made the work hardest was the persistence of his suspiciousness about me.

He said that I reminded him of one of his untrustworthy colleagues. From the beginning, and throughout most of the work, he suspected me of talking to others about him, and laid various traps. He believed that I was somehow exploiting him for his money, and wanted to know much more about my own thoughts than I judged useful. His initial questioning of me never quite stopped. He regarded me as a cold, unfeeling person to whom he could not entrust his deepest thoughts. Interpret though I did the apparent dynamics and origins of these attitudes, they tended to persist, and if there were periods of easing, they were followed, at gradually more obvious moments, by a recurrence of withholding.

I became discouraged. And I asked myself, many times, whether the patient would not be better off with another therapist. Or whether we should decide to terminate. His initial phobic reactions to height, scissors, rooms with closed doors, had abated to some degree, but they were not gone. Otherwise, there was nothing satisfying to point to. On I slogged, assembling myself for the hours with him, one after another. To my surprise, it turned out that my pessimism was ill-founded. He was able to make his life better in many significant ways. Emotional forces set loose in both of us by the decision to terminate resulted in a surge of growth which was to continue in the period following the end. The final chapter of this book is devoted to Dennis Carroll.

In the case of the woman who looked like a bird, Doris Brown, who had moved so many times, and flitted about the office, the middle phase was marked by her attempts, automatic and ingrained, to forget insights that had strong emotional charges. The material of one hour would be lost by the next. She had a special means of escaping from the stresses of therapy. Each spring, she reserved the right to spend three months in a house she owned on the Mediterranean, where her frenetic and confused life would become more tranquil. She asked me how I could object that the time spent there detracted from the work of her therapy. She thought it characterized me as a narrow-minded therapist to think so. And besides, she was willing to pay for her hours, in order to keep them. So why should I object?

To her this retreat was life itself, the chance to enjoy it and to not feel depressed. When she was in therapy, this lively woman would often fall into uncontrollable sobbing. Her life was a waste, her marriage a sham. Why hadn't she continued her medical studies? Why had she succumbed to the lure of her husband's wealth? Why couldn't she hoist herself out of the vacuous social whirl of which she had allowed herself to become an indispensable part? How different she felt in the Mediterranean! There, peace, beauty, harmony reigned. The multicolored garden blown by gentle breezes; the marble terrace where she painted and wrote; the little private beach a few steps down; the charming village where, at one of the three cafés, she could meet everyone in an afternoon. How then, she asked, did I dare make an interpretation to the effect that she was using her annual trip to avoid coming to terms with the underlying depression from which she presumably wished to escape? The first time she reacted this way, I did not respond productively, for I was somehow seduced by her point of view.

But I came to see, very clearly, how she had integrated despair into her life, choosing to suffer to assuage a relentless conscience, and to make deals with herself for self-indulgent sprees and impulsive gestures intended to represent freedom, instead of making a definitive change in her life. In the second year, I vigorously interpreted her plan to go away for three months (she did so anyway). By the third, she was increasingly devoted to the work and decided to stay in town during the spring. I had not questioned the value of the experiences she could have abroad, but only said that their very value was what held her captive, these seemingly unassailable reasons to avoid looking at herself steadily. This was the great turning point in her treatment and her life. She fell into unbearable despair, talked openly of putting a gun to her head, and felt her life to be empty and worthless. Some hours she would not use the couch, and in others she would rush out after ten minutes. Unable to elude the memory of her small-town childhood, she became preoccupied with family scenes in which she had been sadistically teased by her grandfather and made to feel an outcast. Her parents, not rising to her defense, had left her feeling quite alone. Putting aside a great deal of early sorrow, she had moved to London, where she took up with a series of aristocratic men, until she met the person she finally married, an American of middle-class background who was attending an English university.

To her it seemed as if I were aiming to return her to childhood. Yet a gradual understanding took over and the work progressed. I had had to find it possible to deal effectively with her escapes to the Mediterranean to make way for the body of the therapeutic work. This was the substance of the middle phase.

The middle phase is often characterized by the phrase "transference neurosis." Distortions of the relationship to the therapist intensify and life themes intertwine to reproduce the intensity of conflict experienced first in childhood.

Most analysts would say that the transference neurosis, encompassing childhood conflict, is actually a new version of neurosis under the new conditions of analysis. The struggle to deal with it taxes the analyst's ability to retain his own clarity of view, and, when successfully analyzed, always constitutes a major turning point of treatment.

The middle phase can be extremely valuable in teaching both therapist and patient forbearance, which is akin to forgiveness. The therapist attains the role of the one who forgives, not because he sets himself up as a religious or all-knowing authority who can dispense forgiveness, but because he forbears, and does not retaliate for being regarded as so different from what he knows he is. Being misunderstood persistently can feel like violent assault, and sometimes is. The therapist's forbearance is born of many elements, not least the complexly attained capacity to forgive himself, to live with his own limitations, evident day after day, and to continue anyway. He must also be able to imagine something that could be called success in order to face down the difficulties in pursuing a trying and painful course, and this vision of success must come from his own experience, which precedes his encounter with the patient and supports his effort. It is not limited to imagining the patient as improved, for this would foreclose the great range of possibilities. A patient's improved state will often take a form that was unanticipated. Without such a background of hopefulness, the clues given by the patient that suggest the possibility of a good outcome would lose their encouraging quality when the inevitable resistances appear.

The favorable signs derive additional power to sustain by the enhanced meaning that is given to them. The therapist evaluates them in the context of the ongoing process. They leap out of the gray base of free association with a special brightness. The patient who, amidst his usual catalogue of despair, indicates that he could, for the first time, speak up at a professional meeting without trembling and without self-hatred has disclosed a luminous sign that something profound and beneficial is happening. The therapist can now hear of all the ways the patient's life has deteriorated in therapy and not succumb to the patient's mood. The patient who describes that she is remembering the content of her hours for the first time is noticing that she has been affected in a vital way, that, to her amazement, her ability to think can actually improve.

The process of *assigning meaning* is, in itself, a saving grace. It expresses the therapist's capacity to understand how to weigh the various pieces of information that are part of the everyday flood. The patient feels appreciated in an unprecedented way. While it is fair to say that she may have been appreciated by family members in a way she could be by no one else, it is also true that the therapist's scaffolding of thought connects elements that no family member would or could ordinarily join together. This sense of being seen afresh gives hope for a revitalized life. The patient may learn to appreciate her own life by seeing so much more in it than she ever thought was there. Although appreciation and affection are close, they are not identical. I am not speaking of the value of the therapist's liking the patient, but of his grasp of the elements in the patient's life, of his ability to identify what is important, and why. Inevitably, this implies dedicated and sustained attention, and more than that, the articulation of the many features of the patient's life into a functional whole. The patient will never before have been so profoundly understood, nor will the vastness and complexity of her experience have ever been revealed as they are now.

18.

SPECIAL ISSUES

The beginning therapist's tendency to lack flexibility comes from having had to remold himself along the lines taught in training, in order to become a recognizable therapist in the first place. But as the view and techniques he initially brought to his office are found wanting in one way or another in their application to specific cases, he has to learn to modify and supplement them.

I've mentioned the occasional need for the therapist to intervene overtly and swiftly in a patient's life, in contrast to the usual slow evocation and interpretation of the transference. The woman whose child had died, the young woman dying, or the suicidal writer clearly required immediate help. A man who had obvious difficulties with his adolescent children required initially a simple reminder of what is normal for their age. His own father had never provided such understanding of his own similar struggles. Unable to cope at the outset with the distant demeanor of his previous therapist, and reaching out for help, he then required some evidence that therapy could be orienting and useful before he faced deeper issues. I dealt with his subsequent requests for guidance in a less direct fashion, as we shaded into a therapy with less obvious support, which was more productive of interpretable transference.

Situations involving children can make for special pressures on the therapist to intervene. Supposing a mother reports that she is feeding her infant by propping up a bottle in the crib every night, and that one believes, as I do, that this is a serious deprivation of human contact, likely to result in a permanent sense of the world as a lonely place to be, with a related tendency toward withdrawal. It would seem incumbent on the therapist not to let hours and weeks pass waiting for the patient to change. This stage of the infant's development is crucial, and time is of the essence. One might raise the subject by making a comment about the patient's attitude toward the infant, knowing that this will lead to important information. However one does it, the fate of the infant will be involved in the therapy and one's allegiance will be temporarily split between infant and mother.

What are the boundaries of such situations? Suppose that a patient is abusing an adolescent child. The therapist is a human being before he is a therapist, and no pursuit of therapeutic goals can take precedence over a real and pressing danger to anyone else. If a murder or other violent act is a clear possibility, the therapist has a legal as well as a moral obligation to do whatever is necessary to prevent it, though such intervention has been much discussed and disagreed with in the psychiatric community. No therapist wants political and juridical figures entering his office and telling him what to do with his patients. The sanctity of the therapy relationship is compromised, and the attempt to conduct an objective and sustained therapy potentially impossible. Yet the therapist does not operate in a social and moral vacuum.

He must at the same time confront the patient with the question of why it was left to the therapist to intervene—that is, why the patient himself did not see what he was doing and stop. He addresses the meaning of the patient's blindness. To what extent does the patient assume a license to injure, or remain anesthetized to the pain being inflicted, and for what reason? The patient may be dissociated from his own sadism, or seriously lacking in defenses consistent with civilized values (sociopathic), or psychotic, or neurotically uncaring.

Frequently, the principle that therapists are supposed to refrain from imposing their value system on patients is given as a reason to avoid dealing with episodes of dishonesty, and it is an important caution to take into account. But dishonesty may be viewed as a symptom of an underlying disorder. No sustained pursuit of the truth, which is what good psychotherapy must be, can survive without looking at the dissonant relationship between dishonesty in daily life and presumed honesty in the consulting room.

Interventions to protect innocent and vulnerable people, or to address what Leo Rangell, whose writings have opened the subject of integrity to psychoanalytic study, has named "compromises of integrity," are sometimes important aspects of the middle phase of psychotherapy. They can be fruitfully viewed as part of the larger task of keeping hope alive, for both therapist and patient. The therapist's sense of the vitality of his work depends to some extent on confidence that he can deal with phenomena that don't easily qualify as matters for his intervention. His integrity as a human being is at risk if he should practice at the expense of a sense of right and wrong, even as he strives for an objective position that places his values to one side. At the same time, however, to accept dishonesty as a necessity in the patient's competitive world vitiates the strength of therapy, and neglects the truth that psychological as well as moral integrity does not admit of severe compromise. The therapist who tacitly agrees to leave dishonesty out of an analysis is, in effect, colluding with the patient's fractured conscience.

The therapist's very demeanor expresses integrity, reflecting over the long run the extent to which his own inner struggles have resulted in an integration of the whole. He himself is whole or always aiming to become so, and his method is designed to be broad enough to encompass issues of wholeness or its various degrees of fragmentation. His poise, his restraint, his careful judgment, his ability to focus empathy and turn his observations into usable comments, bespeak that process of transformation from layman into therapist which is not merely a matter of learning technique from various sources, but must also include a successful resolution of the struggle to overcome the lies one tells oneself to avoid anxiety and depression. The *presence* that results may be fearful for the patient, as if an Old Testament God were taking a searching look into his deeds and thoughts. The experience for the patient must not be intimidating, which leads to shrinking from or worship of the therapist, so it must be understood in all its ramifications. Many patients do not seek help because they are afraid of being exposed to judgment, and even when they are driven to a therapist by their suffering, they may be determined to withhold certain secrets. The therapist, who knows what it is to struggle to acknowledge one's less admirable wishes and deeds, can feel a kinship with the frightened patient, and does not assume a holier-than-thou stance, or conduct a therapeutic witch hunt. He knows that he can best help the patient to see the ways in which his or her life has been damaged by dishonesty if he can demonstrate the value of honest understanding.

Take a patient who is conniving, insincere, manipulative, given to cheating others, willing to betray his close friend, or, more commonly, unfaithful to his or her spouse. It is likely that under such conditions the therapy itself will eventually become an object of deceit, and the therapist put to a test. The patient may ask that certain false information be put on an insurance form, or that bills falsify the fee. Refusing to do so is the beginning of addressing the patient's ideas about right and wrong.

More subtly, the patient may seek out ways to engage the therapist as a defense against the uncomfortable sense of being the object of close observation. For example, a patient may directly link the payment of his bill to the receipt of money illegally obtained. A patient who deals in cocaine may come in with a check and talk at length about how he obtained it. The point may be made that there would be no therapy without his drug dealing. If the therapist continues to accept money from the patient, is he in some way a collaborator in his illegal dealings? Often the patient would like to think so, and thereby be relieved of the ethical distance that divides them. If faced with a choice between terminating the therapy and continuing it with payment made from illegal activity, which is right? Among the possible dynamics is the patient's sense that nothing good can be "legally" his own, so that he must negate his own opportunity to develop by besmirching the therapist's honesty. This leaves him only able to respect a therapist who refuses to treat him, able to benefit only from what he can never have. Such a line of thinking leads to despair, from the mobilization of a conscience that is actually vicious in the deprivations it enforces, not the permissive one it seems to be.

A patient's son got hold of the school records and falsified a grade. It did not occur to the patient that he might ask his son to admit the act to the school authorities and face the consequences. This would probably have ruined his chances of admission to a particular university. "You have to decide on the greater good," he said to me. A few weeks later he described a complicated arrangement with his business partner, which limited the scheduling of his therapy sessions to late in the day so that he could be in his office during the early morning hours. He did this without discussing it with me, and when I heard about it, I had a number of interpretations to make. He had assumed that I could and would provide him with whatever hours he wanted, as if there were only one person involved in such decisions, and he didn't understand me when I brought this to his attention. On second thought, he said, perhaps he could secretly continue to see me at the same morning times when his partner was out of town, and looking me in the eye, he added: "But wouldn't this be dishonest, Doctor?" His discomfort with the earlier discussion about his son led him to seek a way to throw doubt on my integrity. He recognized that he had to renegotiate his agreement with his partner. The tensions generated by his style of resolving conflicts through dishonesty became an ongoing and fruitful focus of attention.

A patient handed me five hundred dollars in cash and said he was not going to report the payment as a deduction on his tax form, and that I could pocket the money without recording it as income. The taxes I would have had to pay were a gift to me. This sort of easy bribe calls the observant therapist's attention to other ways in which the patient might be acting deviously.

Cheating on taxes is a national pastime, and as such excuses indulging in a bit of harmless larceny. Patients will extend their "justified dishonesty" to corporations whose computers deal impersonally with them. What's wrong with cheating the telephone company? The therapist knows that dishonesty is part of the human situation, on small and large scales, as one part of a person turns away from knowing what another part wants or is scheming to achieve. In the effort to understand the patient, the therapist is always aware of possible distortions because of conflicts of his own. He wants the clearest possible view. He looks at his own dreams and recognizes the clever constructions, the reversals, the ways in which he has attempted to hide the truth behind the dream. And he knows that if a complaisant attitude toward dishonesty enters his life, the tonic effect of full devotion to truthfulness will be aborted and eventually his pride in good work will go.

Like anyone else, the therapist shares in the complications of the human condition. He knows, like those who sheltered Jews in Nazi Germany, or those who defied segregation in the South, that there are times when a lie or resistance to law are the acts of greatest integrity, when fidelity to higher ideals requires that one forgo a more customary honesty, or when honesty demands a clash with otherwise respected authority. He is chastened, in short, by an awareness that right and wrong can be difficult to discern. Should he accept payment from a drug dealer whose emotional problems are part and parcel of his occupation? Or deny him the help? One can sharpen the issues if the patient is selling to teenagers, or even younger children. There is a point for any therapist beyond which he cannot go, in which the disturbance to his own sense of values is great enough to paralyze him as therapist, or to evoke such distaste that the empathic process is impossible. Most of us would have a difficult time helping a Gestapo criminal who tortured thousands, except as a research task. Who, then, deserves our best efforts?

To some extent, the profession of the therapist takes his work out of the personal realm—that is, he can treat people with whom he is not in sympathy. He need not like a patient to be of help, although it is very likely that he will come to see aspects of the patient that he will feel for over the course of a successful treatment. This is so because the tragedy of origins in anyone becomes plainly evident when looked at closely enough. That we do not ask to be born, nor choose our parents or early experiences, and yet are shaped by all this beyond the limits of will to correct it, and are still responsible for being what we are and doing what we do—this is our common lot.

A patient's striving for some good may give the therapist a sense of potential conflict behind dishonest or exploitative behavior and make it possible to see value in treatment. And if a connection can be made between dishonesty and the anxiety that initiated the choice of a dishonest solution but was afterward lost, the therapist is on his way to helping the patient reach for a state of integration.

A woman who enjoyed an occasional indulgence in shoplifting acted as if it were picky of me to make interpretations about it. She was in my office, she said, because her life was boring: shoplifting pepped it up a bit. "The only thing that's fun is breaking the rules," she told me, in all honesty. As I slowly but persistently gathered information about her shoplifting, she began to notice that she experienced the urge under very specific circumstances, always after disappointment with someone close to her. Returning after a month-long vacation, to the announcement of which she had responded with a yawn, I was told how she had been held by the police for an act that she committed on the first day of my absence, during the very hour I would have seen her. Her sense of deprivation brought the symptom into the context of the transference, where, with little difficulty, it was possible to trace it back to the absence of her mother during her early childhood. Her mother's hospitalization for tuberculosis had left her bereft at two and a half. The way she felt at the ends of hours, weekend breaks, and holidays now enabled us to focus carefully on her fluctuating state of anxiety. Consciousness of anxiety replaced impulsive action. Eventually, she recognized conflict and sorted it out, instead of expressing it with self-destructive action.

I've been speaking of the necessity to generate conflict in patients who have grown accustomed to behaving in dyssocial ways. By promulgating a theory that emphasizes conflict among parts of the psyche, Freud has been accused of *contributing* to modern man's sense of fragmentation. Certain analysts, such as Heinz Kohut, suggest that there should be less emphasis on discussions of intrapsychic conflict, where wishes collide with reason and conscience, and correspondingly more recognition of man as a whole person. They believe that the natural bent of analysts toward dissection needs to be redressed by active recognition that the patient is a whole being; and there is value in their recommendations. Yet both points of view remain valid, and there would appear to be no need to give up either one. It is, after all, the dialectical tension in the therapist, who now notices aspects of the patient locked in conflict, and now his principles of coherence, that produces the therapist's perspective. The fragments won't come together unless they can be identified and understood, unless, in some sense, wholeness represents both a potential and an achievement, the result of strenuous resolution. By the same token, the therapist's power derives from his struggle to do justice to all aspects of the patient's *reality,* the final arbiter, not from a saintly effort to dissolve its less appealing aspects.

19.

COMMON TYPES OF PATIENTS
AND THE APPEAL
OF NEW METHODS

Severely *psychotic* patients may require a hospital for treatment, but many can be seen as outpatients if the psychotic
process is under control. A young man with a waxing and
waning set of paranoid delusions came to see me for many
years, once a week. We had a strong relationship, based in
part on my decision to relinquish any strong expectation of
cure. I knew that improvement was a good thing in itself,
whatever was to follow. As a result of our work, he was able
to behave more realistically in finding work and in his relationships with women. There was a great deal of freedom in
our conversation. We drank coffee together and went over
his week and his experiences. When he expressed psychotic
anxiety, I urged him to forget about the delusional preoccupation if he could, that it led nowhere. I had learned through
long experience with him that interpretations were limited
in their calming effect on such anxiety, and that my not
being alarmed by whatever he had to say was quite valuable.
When he was more relaxed, I could reconstruct sequences of
his life, with attention to the link between early experiences
and the later ones that set off his psychosis. I saw his tragic
struggle with a deeply ingrained distorting process, his val-
iant effort to make a life for himself, his unfailing humor, his
intelligence, his remarkable and poetic grasp of the English

language, his care for other people. And I knew that this respect for him came through and that my continuing availability was central to his life. He could call during the week, and I always gave him a phone number when I went away. I did not think in terms of a beginning, a middle, and an end. There had been a beginning, and I had thought there might be an end, but I had given up on it. I hoped he could make a life in which he would not feel the need for me, but I was prepared to be there for the long run. And this attitude, not an attitude of pessimism, but one, strangely, of hope, meant a great deal to him. I had had to give up the usual push for an achievement. He and I were both faced with a basic disturbance of mental function which exceeded our powers, and we became content with doing the very best we could. I had to be resigned to an indefinite middle, where the end could not be imagined. He could only have been further disoriented by the expectation of a cure.

Patients with *character disorders,* whose symptoms tend to bother other people more than themselves, such as uncooperative and argumentative types, or dishonest exploiters such as I described in the last chapter, may seek treatment as they see their life situations deteriorate. Commonly, the spouse threatens to leave unless they get help. Such patients can be very difficult to help, because they want to show that they are not the ones who need treatment.

A woman whose employer said she had to get treatment or be discharged came to me feeling that she had been put under undue pressure. She had been behaving seductively toward another employee, whose wife learned of it. She had done the same on two previous jobs. Her first marriage ended because of an affair with the man next door. She failed to show up for an appointment with me and said, when I called, that she had decided not to come. She couldn't afford it. Two years later, after the end of her second marriage, she called again. This time her treatment lasted four months.

Toward the end she was asking me personal questions and sitting in provocative positions. After yet another two-year break, she was back again, frightened of the approach of her fortieth birthday, and now willing to take a longer look at herself. In the course of a tumultuous treatment during which she often tried to reach me during the night with suicide threats, she recovered a memory of being molested by her stepfather. When she had tried to tell her mother about it, she was ignored. Her manipulative forays into promiscuity stemmed from this event. What she most feared was that I would not prove resistant to her overtures, that she would lose this chance to be understood and not exploited. The work went well. She returned to college to develop a special artistic skill and in time she did achieve a stable intimate relationship.

A man named George Lewis, who had spent his life in constant conflict with authority figures by treating them disparagingly, dealt similarly with me. At first, I heard little of this directly. It was only through his reports of what his friends were saying about his therapy that I was able to see that he must have been presenting me in a most unfavorable light. He would report the entire content of an hour, as he saw it, to a certain friend whose attitude was as cynical as his. The opinions expressed by his friend were then used as support. "You must have had something to do with that opinion," I said. "Your friend must somehow know that you want to hear this sort of thing."

"No," he protested. "I'm neutral about it. I swear it." Dreams, outbursts of irritability with me, snide references to psychoanalysis, were seen in their relation to the conversations with his friend, until he gradually reported them with less distortion, and after some months could see what he was doing. He became much more tense about his treatment. Long silences, and then outbursts of accusations and arrogant remarks made directly to me, were the signs that his feelings were being gathered into the transference. He developed a hand-washing compulsion that alarmed him, and considered that this was the proof that the therapy was harmful. But as I saw it, the development of the neurotic symptom was the inevitable result of the cessation of his character defenses, and made it possible that he could be effectively treated after all. It was the evidence that we had entered the middle phase. The compulsion called our attention to a chronic state of guilt emanating from childhood urges to strangle a younger sister, whom he sometimes assaulted. Complaints about his father's preference for the sister had become generalized as a jaundiced view of anyone in authority. Vocal criticism of them had shielded his own guilt. This patient was able to make use of the insights offered and to contribute to a revitalizing of his marital relationship. All had hinged on his ability to give up a natural tendency to render me useless by depreciation.

Some patients have *rigid character defenses,* not something easily seen as a symptom, as a phobia or an anxiety state or hypochondria is. Typical are individuals with obsessional ways of life, always neat and clean, emotionally unavailable, and often high achievers. Their lives are squeezed dry of fun and spontaneity. They can't get close to others. Dennis Carroll, the lawyer with multiple phobias, was such a man. Such patients do not yield to short-term treatment, and may not respond to treatment of any length. Their emotional unavailability translates into distance from the therapist too. They may understand a great deal intellectually, without having it mean anything emotionally. It is this above all that makes for the problem. Any kind of incident that generates emotion is welcome. If the patient's wife announces, to his chagrin, that she is leaving him, or he is upset by a severe professional reversal, or, against all odds, finds himself in tears over the fate of someone he knows, then a feeling being may be born out of the obsessional ashes. The presence of emotion then energizes the exchanges with the therapist. The evidence of its power to reduce rigid defensive positions makes improvement a possibility after all.

The *hysterical* character presents the therapist with another kind of difficulty. Typically, though not exclusively, such patients are women. Emotional in superabundance, seductive, manipulative, terrified of the aging process, given to suicidal gestures, childish in the need for admiration, such patients often have dramatic courses of treatment. Seemingly responsive to the therapist's ideas, they may return the next day as if nothing of importance had been said. They hardly grasp the suffering of those around them, though a facade of sympathy may sometimes appear. Confronted with a potentially effective therapy, they may bolt. Sometimes, their remote phases suggest an underlying psychosis, with episodes of dissociation. The inner life, seemingly so fantasy filled and lively, is actually impoverished. The seductive woman is really a little girl whose sexuality has not matured. The special difficulty for the therapist is in the impression they make of being highly manipulative. This may create a resentment in him which leads to discounting the seriousness of their problems. The therapist may then regard the patient as having a moral rather than a psychological problem, which is wrong.

A woman in her forties, with a history of plastic surgery and with crisscrossed scars on both wrists, blew into my office for her first session and began quoting sonnets on the subject of the beauties of spring. The vogue for facial makeup permitted her to paint her face vividly, almost grotesquely. Many lovers, maltreatment at the hands of men, suicidal gestures, disappointed ambition—I had heard such stories before. Would I mind letting her use my phone to call her maid? Yes, I would mind. What she required was interpretations, but I had to deal with my own hostility in order to state them. To do this, it was necessary that I find a way to view her behavior as the means by which she was making herself known to me, to see it as not personal at all. This is true of any patient, but the hysteric's provocativeness makes it a difficult task.

Hysterical symptoms, such as loss of voice, blindness, or paralysis, result from a process known as *conversion*, whereby an unconscious conflict is expressed in the body. Physical examination reveals no basis for the symptom, which expresses a conflict symbolically, without regard to anatomical reality. An area of anesthetized skin does not conform to the distribution of a particular nerve, for example. Such symptoms are not as common as they once were, though neurologists probably encounter them more often than psychiatrists. They are often related to the presence of primitive, religiously enforced conscience, such as one finds in fundamentalist groups.

Patients with *alcoholism and drug addictions* are extremely difficult to treat with psychotherapy or psychoanalysis. The use of chemical shortcuts to mood alteration usually proves more than a match for even the most insightful and patient therapist. There is a literature on the analytic treatment of such people, but the work is limited to a tiny handful of research-oriented therapists. These patients seem to benefit most from belonging to groups such as Alcoholics Anonymous, which can provide the kind of support and spiritual sustenance that is required. Therapy as an adjunct may then have a useful role to play.

Patients with *psychosomatic disorders,* such as those with duodenal ulcer, ulcerative colitis, bronchial asthma, and neurodermatitis, are often driven by unsuccessful medical treatment to seek the help of a therapist. Their treatment can be very difficult, and is shadowed by the patient's and therapist's concern that getting into the deeper conflicts will result in a life-threatening attack. A patient with severe dermatitis of the face and upper body had severe flare-ups as if for no discernible reason. The progress of therapy enabled us to see a pattern, connected with extreme sensitivity to "closeness" to me. We had excellent rapport much of the time and it gave me great pleasure to see and help her. The inevitable defenses began to be manifested in outbreaks of her skin disorder. She had been given to rashes as a child, probably an avenue of expression of the emotions that was favored for genetic reasons. She had the pale and sensitive skin of her Irish forebears and there was a history of allergy in the family. The more she learned about herself, however, the more she found it possible to *think* about what bothered her, and the less her skin was a problem. Her symptom was significantly benefited, though not cured.

A category that has received great attention in recent years is that of the *narcissistic personality disorder*. People with this problem are said to be characteristic products of the "me generation," though they may have existed in the same numbers in former days, and went unrecognized. They are self-absorbed and in constant need of support. They fall to pieces, without becoming overtly psychotic, when a person on whom they depend lets them down. They regard certain key people as extensions of themselves, and function only when they are not reminded that the other person has an entirely separate life. The theoretician of greatest note in understanding these patients was the late Heinz Kohut. He advised radical changes in psychoanalytic method, laying special emphasis on the importance of the analyst's continuous empathic immersion in the patient's mental state. Because of such a patient's early problems in achieving an idealization either of a parent or of himself, which is considered indispensable to healthy development, Kohut recommended that the patient's idealization of the analyst should not be aborted by his making interpretations about it. The analyst understands his patient in terms of the development of transference states which reflect the unmet need for idealization. He finds himself sometimes mirroring the nascent grandiosity of the patient or being idealized himself, and he pays special attention to states of fragmentation that follow disappointment with the analyst, who is maintaining the conditions under which developmental gains may be made at long last. Narcissistic problems of a similar type are also thought to be present in a good many other people, whose main symptoms do not suggest the fully developed syndrome.

The greatest spur to a deeper understanding of the nature of the therapist's task is the experience of failure when he has given his best. He tries to be honest with himself about his limitations and mistakes, and to learn from them. Reading the literature, attending professional meetings, consulting with particularly skilled teachers, studying with respected colleagues, provide a continuous stream of information about the experiences of others. Most practitioners are aware of which ideas are in the forefront of consideration at any given time. In the forties and fifties there was a profusion of contributions to ego psychology, led by Heinz Hartmann, Ernst Kris, and Rudolph Loewenstein. In the sixties a book by Edith Jacobson, *The Self and the Object World,* was a focus of discussion. Around that time the appearance of Margaret Mahler's monumental studies of early development called everyone's attention to the value of knowing about symbiosis and individuation in the first few years of life. Piaget's encyclopedic work on cognitive development became indispensable referents for anyone concerned with children. In Los Angeles, confronted by a tide of interest in the work of Melanie Klein, we all became more closely acquainted with her contributions, and the presence of Wilfred Bion, who came from London to be part of our community, introduced us to his baffling and sometimes inspiring writings. Analysts and therapists, to the extent that they are truly involved in their work and are not merely working for a living, naturally evolve in the atmosphere of the times.

There appears to be a tendency among practicing therapists to synchronously alternate in enthusiasm between "hard" and "soft" ideas, those that emphasize the importance of personal responsibility giving way to kindlier visions of man's helplessness, as if the pursuit of one viewpoint eventually exposes its incompleteness and makes way for a wave of enthusiasm for its corrective. William James first called attention to this way of classifying psychological theories in his distinction between "toughmindedness" and "tendermindedness."

For example, the "human potential movement" was propelled by the hope that untapped human resources could be made available on a large scale. It was characteristic of the ethos of the sixties, when expectation of radical change was in the air all over the world. Subsequently, the interest in "est," or Erhard Sensitivity Training, peaked and declined. It featured an emphasis on personal responsibility, and with its sometimes abusive "training sessions" won over many thousands to the view that you hold your fate in your own grasp and can do virtually anything you want to, a version of American romanticism. The height of its popularity, advanced by favorable comments from people in a position to publicize it, such as television actors, coincided in Los Angeles with the zenith of Kleinian psychoanalysis, also a point of view that puts maximum responsibility on the patient.

The followers of Kohut now make an appeal beyond the confines of psychoanalysis, from which their ideas took root. Their larger audience of mental health professionals is addressed in part because the primary arena for the discussion of psychoanalytic ideas in the United States, forums sponsored by the American Psychoanalytic Association, do not appreciate Kohut on the scale his followers believe appropriate. They turn elsewhere because they believe they are saving psychoanalysis from what they consider its narrow preoccupations with the theory of conflict over instinctual drives as an explanation for neurosis.

Problems of narcissism presently command the interest of anyone trying to make sense out of contemporary times. Many patients who seek treatment have been raised without traditional rules or values. Their parents, too concerned with their own immediate pleasures, were unable to maintain sufficient continuity of love and caring to help their children to develop fully. Trapped in a state of self-absorption and suffering, they come to the analyst's office, cynical about psychoanalysis but with nowhere else to go. The Kohutian analyst claims to understand best the defects in their development. Most analysts would point out that the capacity to empathize is not the sole possession of the followers of Kohut, and that his treatment recommendations do not warrant the formation of a new subdivision of psychoanalysis.

A public relations effort to popularize Kohut's thinking contaminates the question of what his theory is worth. Continuing education requirements for holders of state licenses to practice, and membership in groups that might generate personal and professional contacts, contribute to the creation of a social phenomenon, the effects of which will have to be set aside for real scrutiny to occur. The interest and rejoicing with which a new theory is greeted must be subject to careful consideration. The intensity of responsiveness to its appearance, which may indicate that a real need is being addressed, must be examined in the light of which need it might be. Is it purely a matter of what a difficult class of patients requires and has never received? Or is it instead, or in addition, a need in the therapists themselves, such as a rationale for regarding themselves as more giving, or a view of human nature as more basically positive than the Freudian theory implies? Or is it a need to justify the gratification of patients instead of subjecting them to the deprivation that analysis in its traditional form entails? Any phenomenon such as this deserves the respect of prolonged questioning if its kernels of truth are to be culled out. When therapists who would like to be regarded as equal in skill to analysts are directly addressed by analysts dissatisfied with their reception from peers, something more is being offered and responded to than a series of discoveries. The Kohut phenomenon is only a single example of an irrational accompaniment of the presentation of potentially discussable ideas. The slow work of testing those ideas will finally tell us which belong to the psychology of professional groups and which should become part of psychoanalytic technique.

20.

ENDINGS

If the patient's defenses have proved to be surmountable, then out of the persistent work of the middle phase develops a logical and convincing version of his development, a context for the symptoms that led to treatment. It is reconstructed from multiple sources. The *transference* will have presented an avenue of observation of the past as it is manifested in the present. The patient's changing view of the therapist will have guided the growing comprehension of the history of the patient's experiences and attitudes. Memories of the past will be seen in the new light of the therapist's vision and the patient's response to it. What had stood isolated and fragmentary now assumes significance as part of the whole.

The dramatic appearance of *recovered memories* adds information that is especially convincing and useful. Well into the treatment, as a rule, often just before the closing phases, the patient sometimes remembers a long-forgotten event. Or he remembers a new detail in an old memory, which alters his view of its meaning. This sudden reacquaintance with the past provides links for previously baffling ideas about the true events of childhood. The fact that memories can actually be recovered vindicates the process of therapy, and all the painstaking attention to defenses. The reappearance of lost memory confirms the forward thrust of the treatment and contributes to it. The feeling that the complexion of things may suddenly change for the better is related to the lifting of repression and consequent recovery of a part of the self that had been repressed along with memory. That there is more to one's life than one knew leads to the invigorating idea that there is more to life itself than one had realized.

A third major source of material with which the past is reconstructed is the *therapist's inferences* about it. Given his absorption in the process of reconstruction right from the beginning, he can in time provide the logical links that do not spontaneously appear. He must avoid wild guesses or premature inferences, or the stance of one who can *recreate* the patient's life. Biding his time, he offers his ideas on appropriate occasions, and the patient most often responds with relief and encouragement. The process is akin to the reconstruction of ancient artifacts out of shards. The knowledgeable archaeologist can provide the necessary transitional materials and shapes, and as he does so, an incomplete vision of the past gradually makes its appearance. The vision is worked over and tested through many versions, altered to fit first this and then that new bit of data, until something reasonable and sturdy develops to replace the previous, much less accurate one. In a sense, the reconstructed life summarizes all of importance that took place in therapy, for it includes insights available through a study of the transference, through understanding the defenses, and through recovered memories.

The therapist becomes acutely aware of the shifts in his own functioning over time, and knows instinctively when the patient's defenses are not hindering the work. The sequence repeats itself throughout the therapy, periods of defensiveness followed by periods of relaxed opening up, as the acquisition of insight with an accompanying ease of communication leads to the newest area that the patient must defend. Free association waxes and wanes accordingly. But the therapist, better and better acquainted with the patient, as the patient becomes less and less able to hide from what both he and the therapist know, can more quickly supply the needed interpretations, and do so with language that condenses a great deal. The evolution of his capacity to summarize on many levels marks the growth of the therapeutic process. His choice of words permits explicit expression of the main idea, combined with wide-ranging implications for underlying ones. A sarcastic woman whose mother had weaned her early interrupted me frequently and launched into extended revisions of what I had begun to say. I said it was as if she bit off a piece of me, and quickly chewed it up to make it her own. This made it difficult for her to receive the full amount being offered, and must have been frustrating. I had in mind feeding behavior, of course, the infant biting at the nipple before it could be withdrawn. Such metaphors reflect the therapist's thought and prepare for fuller explication of the meaning, if the patient responds.

Selma Miller, who had been adopted and felt that she had never been adequately mothered in life, was difficult to deal with during a long therapy. I had been first provoked to anger by a variety of arrogant poses and histrionic gestures intended to depreciate my efforts. I had been inundated by a strange sleepy boredom as her language deteriorated in the midst of a clinging closeness which excluded clear interchanges of ideas. And whenever it had seemed we were making excellent progress, she had punctured it by saying that she was exactly the same as she had been at the beginning, that nothing of value had happened. But I was encouraged by my own perceptions of her growth, knowing of her doubt about ever being able to overcome the events of her birth. She became better able to wait and think before indulging in habitual defenses. She became more reflective and willing to consider various possible explanations for her behavior. Although she occasionally continued to depreciate me, she did so less often and only under particularly trying circumstances.

Then, in the third year, Mrs. Miller noticed that the end of every hour was marked by a sudden loss of energy. She could hardly raise herself off the couch. She dragged herself between the couch and the door, gradually recovering energy in the hallway outside the office, and in five minutes' time was back to normal. I thought these episodes added new understanding of the clinging behavior that had contributed to her three divorces. She had kept me at a distance by depreciating what I offered, defending against the disappointment that was regarded as inevitable if she took up a clinging attitude. She would not permit herself to be seduced by what she believed was really false—that is, what, as she understood it, an adopted mother gives. Now she was struggling against separation. She had been receiving what she needed, something real, consistent, and pertinent. And the sense of loss was translated into a weakened bodily state at the end of the hour.

Having indicated that her parents had let her know about her adoption when she was quite young, that she seemed to have always known about it, she now became preoccupied with the early years. One day she told me a dream, in which she was in a jail, listening to a conversation going on somewhere outside the bars. There was someone else in her cell, someone who looked very much like another patient of mine, whom she had recently seen entering the waiting room as she left. She felt vaguely uneasy about her.

She then talked about a house to which her family moved when she was four years old. There she had a large room of her own. But before that she had shared a room with her sister, who was three years younger. Her sister had been her parents' natural child. Then, in the midst of her associations, there was a change in the tone of her voice. She became intent, concentrated. "I think I can remember my old room," she said. "I can remember how the light came into the room in the afternoon and made a shadow on the wall." The shadow showed the bars on the side of a crib. The crib must have belonged to Susan, her sister. "I think I must have known that she and I had different parents about then. I must have heard something. Perhaps my parents told me. I think that in the dream I was listening for information about this subject, trying to understand how it could be that I was adopted and she wasn't." The intent listening, associated with the early age, made me think that she was concerned with what the parents did when they were alone, and what their noises might have had to do with creating babies. And I reflected on the meaning of the periods in treatment when I found myself sleepy, when her language deteriorated, having seen in other cases the association between such states and fantasies of what Freud called the primal scene.

My other patient represented the new baby that had crowded her out. In the ensuing weeks, preoccupied with the idea that I liked the other patient more than her, she was able to move between being convinced of this and reflecting on the meaning. She was now able to make use of the experience of transference by grasping its significance without my help.

Working through this, Mrs. Miller came to value what I had been offering her as genuine, not less than what I gave the other patient, and began to forgive her adopted parents, who also had done the best they could. She grew interested in her own biological parents for the first time, and she thought she might try to find them. Her understanding of her own children, previously unreliable, became deeper and more consistent. The clinging behavior that had caused such difficulty in her life—insistence that her husband call her several times a day, watching him every second at social occasions, going to sleep in fear that she would lose him through either death or infidelity—all this declined. Major personality revisions were in progress, signaled by the recovered memory, furthered by the ongoing therapy process.

During this period it became possible to understand why her maternal attitudes were sometimes shallow and competitive. She was able to provide the basics for her children, including genuine love, on occasion. At other times, she was alarmed by an absence of caring, and had to substitute something that would pass for it, such as a little extra allowance. Her rivalry with her younger sister and her jealousy of what she was receiving had been translated into her relations with her own children. Sometimes, they were the means by which she experienced, for the very first time, the biological attachment of mother and child; at others, they were the stimulus to arousing the old, unresolved resentment of her sister.

Renewed contact with her sister led to long reminiscences of childhood, and the discovery of the sister's view of it. Her sister had not been able to get close to her in childhood, warned off by her coldness. Mrs. Miller now came to see how much she had contributed to her own isolation, which was not simply an inevitable consequence of having been adopted but also the result of her own profound disappointment with her condition. The reformulation of her version of her life consistent with recovered information eased her depression and gave her an appreciation for the present.

Changes such as these are the outcome of a process that begins with insight and ends with "working through," by which is meant repeated awareness of an insight in its many applications. Knowing something is not enough. It has to be felt and applied, and revisions of feeling must follow. Patients have to be reminded of what they have learned, many times. And finally, some kind of action often becomes the integrating element, the "doing" that announces that the learning has had a decisive effect. One day Mrs. Miller decided to share her adolescent diaries with her sister. The two spent many enjoyable hours discussing the feelings and incidents that had once meant so much to them. Mrs. Miller found it possible to laugh at her youthful foibles and was rewarded in turn by her sister's openness about herself. They became kin in spirit for the first time.

This is different from "acting out," a phrase that is applied to behavior which drains transference emotion out of therapy. George Lewis, the patient who depreciated me to his friend, was acting out the transference, instead of manifesting his feeling directly to me. Until he could do that, there was no way to understand it. What he had presented to me was only a piece of the total picture. In contrast to acting out are those healthy actions that are the result of change and that simultaneously solidify it. The decision to take a six-month leave of absence from his job as a shop foreman, in order to write the novel that had been brewing in his mind for years, was the fruit of a patient's progressive relaxation of rigid defenses. His priorities had changed. He decided not to postpone indefinitely the pleasure and risk of writing. This step was vastly different from Mrs. Brown's annual Mediterranean trip, which was largely defensive.

Once these life-exploring and life-enhancing actions have begun to appear, the end of treatment cannot be far off. The long incubation period is probably at an end. An integrated person is leading his life. The regressive work of therapy, in which the roots of conflict have been identified and traced backward to origins, all taking place within the therapist's continuing conception of a whole person struggling to live, has been done.

The quest for a radical revitalization of life is the search for a way to replace old defenses with new or more flexible ones which permit more of the patient's potential for life to be realized. Central to this change is the lifting of repressive barriers. Remembrance of repressed things past is akin to resurrection.

21.

COUNTERTRANSFERENCE
AND
TERMINATION

The therapist is always concerned with differentiating what comes from within himself and what comes from the patient. One reason is that his interpretations, to be correct and effective, must be based upon the *patient's* life, and not be encumbered by his own projections and wishes. He observes directly by listening to the facts and indirectly by observing his own emotional states and extrapolating from them to the conditions in the patient that may have stimulated them. He has a critical view of his empathic knowledge, taking into account the possibility that what he feels is at least partly indigenous to himself, not the result of emanations from the patient. If he can identify what comes from within, he is then left with what probably came from without, and is positioned to think what it might signify.

I felt inspired by my insight into a certain patient and presented it enthusiastically, only to be met with dismay. The patient sensed something similar to his domineering father, trying to instill his own values in his depreciated and disappointing son. I began to see that though I did not intend this, my enthusiasm had been a response to seductive uncertainty in the patient, which had engendered a kind of rejoicing in me when something new and organized could be communicated. I had become a part of the father relationship, unwittingly and quickly. I realized that other patients don't feel this way, and there was nothing especially overbearing in the way I offered my insights to this patient. But I now knew that I must pay special attention to my manner and words when interpreting what he was saying.

The patient reminded me of someone I knew, who was raised by a depreciating father. I recognized the silliness, the lack of self-confidence, the surviving childish smile, the jokes that didn't quite come off. And I had learned from another patient who engaged in a long struggle with his distant and unavailable father that something essential isn't there, that there is an unspeakable loneliness in such circumstances. And I had also learned, from yet another patient, that the urge to hold out hope for an eventual recognition by the distant father can persist without end, with the result that chronic dependency, a sense of impotency in the person himself, can vitiate all his efforts to gain control of his life. Triangulated by multiple points of reference, I was in a position to see the interaction with this latest patient clearly. Alert to signs of the meaning of my interventions, I had no difficulty in monitoring myself. I could easily focus on my own mood as an indicator of the transference. Having seen the dismay produced by the initial set of interpretations, I could guard the level of my enthusiasm. I could infer the fluctuations in the patient's mind from the confusion and clarity in my own, and my impression of the patient as vaguely disgusting weakling versus struggling and suffering adult was the ore that I could then process into useful statements.

As I was better able to delete the traces of provocative force in my commentary, I could see the patient's irrational responses with clarity. And when I spoke of them as descendants of responses originally related to the father, I did so with the knowledge that I had not stimulated them in any way. The issue was sharpened. And the patient, however disoriented, was then dealing with a less cluttered field. He saw the difference between being provoked by something logically supportable (my possibly excessive enthusiasm), and feeling provoked in the absence of an adequate stimulus. And this was the beginning of wisdom. He was on his way to a grasp of the principle of the past in the present.

This is a simple example of the therapist's attention to his own associations as a source of information about the patient. Some analysts consider the entire mass of the analyst's responses to be countertransference. However, the more traditional use of the term is limited to instances in which the therapist's unresolved neurotic problems are touched off by something about the patient's life, appearance, or behavior. The patient may remind the therapist of his own mother, father, or other important figure, to a degree that precipitates feelings and behavior inappropriate to the therapy process. The therapist's ability to think may be clouded by a line of fantasy. Traditionally, such a situation has been regarded as entirely an interference, but some see it as both an interference and an opportunity, a possible source of information about the patient.

A young therapist whom I treated was working with a professional man twelve years his senior. He was unable to listen to his patient's descriptions of his sexual activities without making premature interpretations which stopped his patient short. The man reminded him of his father. When given access to such intimate information the therapist felt that he was transgressing, that he was, in effect, entering the parental bedroom. His clever, quick interpretations were unconsciously intended to change the subject, to remind his patient that the therapist (the little son) was listening to his sexual activity, and to call attention to himself as an object of admiration, who should not be forgotten by his absorbed patient. His supervisor tried to heighten his consciousness of this process, and in the treatment with me, material relating to his father poured forth. The interrupting interpretations appeared to represent attempts to stop the intercourse being described. The therapist's relation to his father had been stormy, the powerful father having treated his son with a firm hand, and the son struggling against the father's dominance, preoccupied, in the typical way of the five-year-old, with castration. The therapist learned a good deal about countertransference in this way, was able to clear the field of much of his own tendency to interfere, and to render assistance to his patient.

The patient's mental process during the effort to describe his sexual life was constantly interrupted by what he construed to be the voice of conscience, which amounted to his mother telling him that what he was doing was wrong. His therapist's interference not only took on meaning for the patient; it was, as well, an enactment of a process in the therapist, who, with this enhanced understanding, was greatly strengthened in his conduct of therapy.

A student of mine was working with a physically attractive woman in her twenties and was stimulated every time he saw her. He found it difficult to listen to what she was saying. It was notable, as well, that in all the case material there were no references to sex. The student's own erotic life had remained unsatisfying. A discussion of these elements provided the student with a perspective from which to examine his state of mind. When he called the patient's attention to the absence of sexual content, she breathed a sigh of relief and said: "That's really the problem. I've never been able to have intercourse." The previous, symptomatic response of the student, probably showing the effect of his patient's powerful inhibitions on his frustrated state, gave way to normal listening and open discussion of the patient's problem. The coming to light of a nearly incestuous relationship to her older brother implied the possibility that the patient had responded to the student in the beginning as if he were the brother with whom she was about to become intimate. He was stimulated by her anticipatory excitement and anxiety. In the subsequent unraveling of the components, he could recognize that the verbal intercourse of therapy was being experienced as a variant of the sexual intercourse that frightened the patient so.

Another patient, a physician herself, spoke hardly at all. She was confused and frightened much of every hour. Along with this, she seemed to communicate with her eyes, subtly signaling to me, as if the two of us shared a secret and I could understand her hints. One day she talked about a research acquaintance who was doing well on a project. She said he was "really humping away," and far be it from her to call him on the telephone. She thought any interruption would stop his progress. I called her attention to the phrase, which she hadn't consciously associated with sex. At this, my own associations went to the fact that she had been born with a severe abnormality of the legs, which required that she wear corrective braces for many years. Her parents divorced three years after her birth, and had often argued about her. I thought of the way she presented herself, with manners that were ever sensitive to the rights of others, as in the instance at hand. Her subtle signaling to me, in the midst of fear, was probably all she could do, all that she felt was permitted, to communicate directly, as if she were a prisoner receiving a visitor on the other side of a thick piece of glass. I now speculated on a connection between her understanding of the conditions in effect around her birth and thereafter, and the conditions in effect in my consultation room. I thought she believed that she had interrupted her parents' relationship by having been born, and that the problem with her legs had been the principal factor in the dissolution of their marriage. The phrase "humping away" suggested to me a childhood recollection of her parents having intercourse, a form of relating that left her completely aside, perhaps especially because of the braces which inhibited her movement. I thought she would have wanted to call their attention to her, and believed, later on, that the attention she required was enough to bring about a permanent interruption, a divorce. I thought she was guilt-ridden as a result, and dealt with this guilt through self-effacement and kindliness. The therapy situation, unmitigated by social exchange, probably made way for a pure sense that she was occupying my time at someone else's expense, that she had split "us" apart. She was being courteous by not saying much to me— that is, not putting too much of a burden on me. In addition, she was probably so anxious that she couldn't think clearly.

I was glad to be reflecting in such organized terms, which, though preliminary, subject to correction and revision, were still evidence of a productive process. I knew that such ideas would take years for her to clarify and make conscious, even if correct. The defenses against knowing them would naturally be formidable. But I could begin to imagine a path leading to major change. Freed of irrational guilt, she would have a life of her own, with fulfillment in the context of a relationship that had so far escaped her. In fact, after several years of an inability to communicate, which threatened to make continued treatment impossible, the patient gradually expressed her state of alarm at the primitive aggressive and erotic urges that were stimulated in the transference. As she encompassed the energies these impulses represented, she was able to present a clear picture of her dynamics, which basically proved that my initial formulation was correct.

The psychotherapist stations himself to respond to cues and influences from the patient. He is "up close," where he can feel what he is meant to feel, and thus can respond to whatever in the patient wishes to make him be something other than himself. He offers himself as clay to be molded, while he observes the molding, and draws conclusions about it. When he loses perspective, he is being taken over by a countertransference process that will require resolution. His work involves communicating observations of the molding process to the patient.

The therapist tolerates being misconceived. He does not retaliate for being regarded as hurtful or mean or indifferent or exploitative. When the patient says that the therapist seems to have deliberately acted like a despised father, the therapist does not tell him that he was not pulling strings, that this is not the sort of person he is, even when he feels a pressing need to do so, to rid himself *immediately* of the burden of accusation. He talks of how frightening it probably is for the patient to think that someone he trusts is playacting, how confusing not to know when you can trust what is said and when not. The therapist's tolerance is a special virtue, unlike any other in any other profession. One may inwardly protest at being regarded as hurtful, when making every effort to help. Or at being told that nothing of value has happened, when one has not only tried hard for a long time but seen evidence that substantial change has occurred.

His state of restraint, forswearing the use of the patient for his own ends, the protracted disciplined stance, including even the enforced bodily stillness, take a toll on the therapist. Yet, even though worn down by being repeatedly misapprehended in the transference, he grows stronger and more determined the more the process deepens. He is lending himself for a purpose, which vindicates his own capacity to bear stress for a greater good. The appeal of his own ideals draws out the best in the patient. The therapist maintains a reliable and continuing framework, while the patient gradually brings to light all the ways in which he has felt guilt without knowing it. Sometimes the guilt is easily identified. At other times, it emerges as fear of the therapist's opinion —the conscience experienced as an external force. Eventually, seeing in perspective the childish distortions that have stamped an entire life with inhibition, self-destructiveness, or other symptoms causes them to lose their power to influence. A new freedom is born.

This is no ordinary confession, conscious sin absolved. No absolution is offered. But, in effect, the therapist's ability to bear being distorted has made it possible for the patient to be relieved of guilt and to live. The therapist has lent his mind to the patient as an extra location which permits the conflicts to be spread out. He has undergone projective processes, unwanted parts of the patient somehow being put into him, and he has accepted and examined what has been put there. He has listened to the equivalent of a squalling and desperate infant, understood the signal, and responded with words that would transform bursts of anguish into communicable sentences.

This process is akin to the way a mother receives whatever is expelled by her infant, particularly the emotions of fear and confusion, and, through her own internal processes and actions, makes the world safe and clear. The restoration of a new, undisturbing world reinforces the infant's faith and trust, and relieves him of the feeling that if he externalizes what is within, which he must do, then he will destroy what he most needs. His most violent projections are met with an adequate outlet, where they may be transformed, soothed, and symbolically "reasoned with."

The therapist doesn't have to want him as a friend to care for his patient's fate. Seeing into the life before him, he will inevitably appreciate something of the condition of one who is likely to be his own worst enemy, and knows that we all share certain human traits. Stimulated both by the patient as a person and by the problem that tests his skills, he applies himself, in every session. Sometimes the patient takes the end of the hour or a vacation break as evidence of stinginess. The patient is shocked that this really isn't his wished-for mother or father. But in the regressed pocket of time that is the recurrent therapy arrangement of sessions, there is room for this resentment. The therapist is often glad to see the session end, glad not to have to receive the patient's projections, glad to have a vacation. He needs the limits. And he needs his own life.

Whatever the theoretical position of the analyst, the patient learns from him to do the work. From the pitch of intense conflict at the heart of it, when the patient's transference neurosis is often matched by a conflict in the therapist which could be called a countertransference neurosis, a descent into reduced tension and increased cooperation marks the oncoming end. The therapist is seen more and more as an ordinary person. However interesting and enjoyable the sessions between these now old acquaintances continue to be, one or both is bound to think seriously of calling it quits.

In an important sense, the ultimate criterion of termination is: *Has the patient resumed development?* It is not whether all the problems have been solved, but that there is a prospect of reasonable change in time, without further therapy. Therapy cannot be a way of life, only an aid to development.

A young woman whom I discussed in Chapter Seventeen, Charlotte Bernard, whose development was retarded in adolescence by her inability to let the relationship to her father recede in favor of a new attachment to a young man with whom she could share an intimate life, began to see that she had lost her ability to know what she liked, because such an ability would have led to an open-ended series of changes which would inevitably have drawn her into a life of her own. This knowledge came after a few months of three sessions per week and, together with other insights, resulted quickly in a visible change. Dramatic changes in her appearance from self-effacing to vibrant were reflected immediately in a spate of overtures from eligible men. She thrived, but also became extremely sad as she saw what was taking place. Thoughts of how much more work might now be done competed with ideas of termination, in both patient and therapist. But the overriding fact was that a developmental thrust had come into being. Because it was necessary that she leave the city, the patient and I agreed to terminate in four weeks. There was time enough to review the short course of treatment, to allow a brief opportunity for new problems to express themselves. I was proud of the work, and sad that I would no longer be seeing this patient. I had daughters of my own and had had practice in celebrating each new victory of theirs, and in bearing the growth of their lives away from mine. I had reaped that special combination of joy and sorrow in my state of restraint as a father, and was, at the time of this therapy, still doing so. The father countertransference made me feel more than a purely objective therapist. Perhaps it was a sine qua non for an effective piece of short-term work with this patient.

There are certain patients for whom your life experiences prepare you especially well, when what you know from having lived it can be made useful to someone who comes into your office from her own context. This patient, somewhat older than my girls, could benefit from what I knew. The extra, silent welcome she probably received from me, the controlled circumstances of a limited therapy arrangement which made for significant exchanges that fathers and daughters would not find possible, redounded to her benefit. I could somehow let her know by the example of my effectiveness and my willingness to "let her go" that a girl can leave her father behind and he will be all right. She and he can both have their lives, must have them, though there is grief at parting. I did not speak such words, nor did I ever mention my own daughters, but I believe she lived out with me a brief reenactment of the conflict over leaving her father. Of course, in all psychoanalytic kinds of therapy, there is anonymity. But the more immediately accessible the information that is being withheld, the more charged with possibilities the exchanges become. The therapist's feelings are ordinarily further afield. When he is in possession of such a wealth of idea and emotion, the words available to him assume an intense coloration and depth that are otherwise attained only at widely scattered moments. In a long-term therapy with Charlotte Bernard, the advantages of my own situation would have been the less, I believe, for its complementary relevance to hers would have diminished in the deeper light of the work. What was different would doubtless have been more important than what was similar.

Selma Miller, whose adopted condition had meant so much in her life, approached the subject of her mother in the transference, showing an array of defenses as she went. Fearful of putting herself in a position to forget that I was only a therapist, not a real mother, she responded to every break in continuity, and every interruption of my empathic understanding, with a regression to profound disappointment, usually masked by arrogance, silence, and provocation. It took years of dealing with these situations before she acquired sufficient understanding to observe the process as it was happening, and to put into words all of what she felt. One sign of the change was that she occasionally fell asleep on the couch. At first angry at this "waste of time," she gradually allowed herself the replenishment these naps afforded. She was, in effect, sleeping in my arms, the arms of the mother she longed for. Dreams of good experiences replaced the basically indecipherable ones of earlier phases. These periods of tranquillity were punctuated by recurrences of her old disquiet. Just when I thought I could discern a continuous line of change, she would tell me that these naps of hers and my tolerance of them were nonsense. What could come from sleeping through a session? Nothing!

It was sophistry to think otherwise. What about more insight, what about more direct verbal support? Why did I refuse to encourage her when she was having trouble with her husband and with her self-esteem? But I had learned to see these comments as transient efforts to deal with the pull of regression. If I had supplied the sort of remarks she wanted, she would have been momentarily freed of the transference version of me as the depriving mother. Instead she desperately needed to come to terms with it.

On the couch she dreamed of an enormous blimp floating across a summer sky. She was awed by the size, the shape, and the silence. There were a number of children on board, enjoying an outing. It was a birthday party. Then the blimp began to descend, vaguely frightening, but she quickly saw that the intent was that she come along too. She was hoisted into the cabin, welcomed by the group. A kindly man and woman were in charge. They smiled warmly at her. Somehow she recognized them and she liked them. In fact, she loved them. It turned out that the birthday party was for her. They spent an afternoon moving over the city, enjoying themselves. She awoke with a smile and a sense of peace.

The sense of belonging, of a welcome birth, of parent figures whom she loved, brought together a number of deep and chronically frustrated wishes. The dream was an overview. The blimp reminded her of a breast. She could understand the relationship between being nourished with food and being nourished by persons who loved her. The dream marked a change, for after this there were no more outbursts and a gradual integration began; she became a consistent and reliable companion to her husband and a much more generous mother. She returned to a university to pursue the degree she had not obtained many years before. The end of her therapy was near.

I had a nourished feeling of my own. I felt not only that I had provided her with the conditions for change, that I was exhausted by the restraint and understanding and forbearance required of me, but that I, too, had been given a gift. I suppose it is the mother's feeling when the infant feeds and grows. My skills had been put to a severe test. I had not been taught what to do with such patients, but had been able to combine what I had learned from treating other patients with what I had read and heard, and then invented the rest. I was being vindicated, as a person and as a therapist. Wherever this woman went now, she would take what I had been able to give her.

Toward the end, someone made a gift to me of a tree for my office. When she saw it, she thought perhaps *I* had changed. Feeling that I now wished to be responsible for a living thing made her glad. Somehow my changing was related to her changing. She could not have changed unless I did. And she was right, in a way. I had had to learn to bear more assault, more disappointment, more retraction of the good feelings than I commonly experienced. I had had to learn to shape myself to her needs, while surviving and growing in my own life. So we *had* both changed. Yet what she meant at the heart of it was that I had responded to her. She could not have attained integration without the sense that I had recognized her well by making room for her in my life. The tree was the symbolic means by which she expressed herself, through fantasy. She integrated it into a version of what my experience with her had meant to me, using the tree as a person uses experiences of the day before as raw material for the construction of a dream. As she left my office for the very last time, she took a few seconds to stare quietly at the tree.

Doris Brown, who looked like a bird, and who used to spend every spring near the Mediterranean, responded to my interpretations of her running away from therapy and self-confrontation by staying home and getting severely depressed. As we were able to see that her despair had taken root in a complex childhood fantasy that emphasized the supposedly destructive effects of her emotionality on her parents, especially her mother, she began to improve. The struggle manifested itself in an inability to lie on the couch, where she felt that all her defenses were removed. To fly like a bird was her idea of the good life, meaning to constantly overcome an inner process that tended to immobilize her. This visualization of depression as "being down" put me in the position of one who wanted her to be depressed. It seemed that my whole aim as a therapist was to make her more and more depressed, while she, who had had enough of that, beginning with suicidal thoughts in childhood, wanted to be "up." As her defenses against being understood were analyzed, she could experience more fully what had been there all along, though avoided in the constant motion of her schedule, her moving from place to place. And just when she experienced a marked surge of real improvement, which was not based on a flight from depression, she had an automobile accident that nearly ended her life. Driving late at night, and having had too much to drink, she missed a freeway turnoff and rammed her car into a signpost. She fractured her skull.

The result of her apparent carelessness was appalling, and reinforced what I had long known, that periods of improvement are often accompanied by the special risk of a self-destructive act. It is as if the person does not feel he deserves the better life, the fuller life, and punishment is meted out by an outraged conscience bent on reestablishing its primacy. Its angry and controlling aspect is in danger of dissolution and, like a depreciated authority, is bent on demonstrating its power. Luckily, my patient escaped without permanent damage. When she resumed her treatment, several months later, she was a chastened and frightened person. Once again, she viewed me and the therapy as aiming to undo her, and it was only with great persistence and gentleness that I could show her that she had been living all along as if under a sentence of death, should she dare to reach for more than money could buy. Her accident was no accident, but the work of conscience, invisible as long as the extent of her development was limited, suddenly apparent when development thrust forward. Slowly, and carefully, she was able to recapture the thread of thinking that had been cut by the accident.

I had had to deal with my own concerns about what I was doing to her. Even knowing, from prior experience, the nature of the stakes, I had to review for myself the value and appeal of her previous effort to deal with hopelessness by arranging for "good times" wherever she could find them, versus the possibilities, good and bad, in deeper understanding. At moments, I thought it was too much to subject her to, this underlying despair. But in the silence of my reverie, she took up the task of free association, less hindered by talk from me. And I could see then that she wanted very much to proceed.

Six years after the end of her analysis, I encountered Mrs. Brown in a shop near my office. She looked extremely well, vigorous, in good humor. Throwing her arms around me after an initial hesitant moment while she made out who I was, she broke into laughter and told me that she had practically forgotten that she had once been a patient in analysis. She said that she and her husband, with whom she is on very good terms now, spend six months or so in Europe each year, that she paints seriously there, and conducts art classes for the village children. "And I'm at peace with myself," she said, as if divining my question. She described a long process of remodeling her home and garden in California, and the pleasure it had brought her. I thought of the changes that had been going on within, of course, speculating on the relationship between what she had been doing and what she had been feeling. She told me with pride something about her son's and daughter's lives as well. I could see in her face, now somewhat more lined than when I had known her, that she did have a more natural, less tense look. I felt in good contact with her. We were both older now, and I wondered how I looked to her.

22.

AFTER

TERMINATION

I saw Dennis Carroll standing in front of the restaurant from across the street, and waved. He smiled back, a tall man, slightly overweight, wearing a dark blue suit, a professional at midday. How different he looked from the first time I had seen him, when he questioned me about myself, and was then practically paralyzed by anxiety. Now there was a certain ease of movement, an evident absence of fear. We shook hands, looking briefly and searchingly into each other's eyes, and entered the restaurant. While we waited for our orders to be taken, he started to tell me that during the previous fourteen months he had often had the idea that he should have opened up more when he was seeing me. I thought about it a moment and told him that it was a little like life as a whole, with all the regrets one has when one realizes that one hasn't made the most of it, all those minutes and hours and days when opportunities were not seized, and time passed away into oblivion.

He listened, shook his head, and muttered: "Isn't that something." I could feel a measure of value being added to my cliché, and knew that the positive transference was still present.

I was there in response to his expressed wish to see me, but also because something in me wanted to see him. I thought I was simply curious, that I wanted to know firsthand what happens after treatment is over, but I liked him too.

He had chosen a very small table in the corner of the room. My side was cramped by proximity to a wall behind me. It meant that I could not move my chair far away from the table and get the right distance for comfort. I would have to be close. I wasn't used to it with patients. It prevented me from taking refuge out of his immediate range.

He had mentioned on the phone that there were moments when, riding in his car alone, he thought of me and of all he had received from the treatment, and he would cry. "I'm still grieving," he said. The emotion he described had appeared near the end of the six years of treatment.

I looked into his steel-blue eyes, set deep into a longish, almost funereal face, his big teeth visible in a semi-smile that showed his discomfort and uncertainty, and I noticed that I did not turn away. I sensed the immanence of a kind of bright, flashing scotoma in my visual field as I looked into his eyes, from which I felt it might be necessary to turn my gaze, as if seeing him could trigger a migraine but it wasn't quite there. The years behind the couch, with the soft comfort of the dark distance, had not, in this case, turned him into a dangerous sun which I would feel compelled to avert.

The very fact that we sat vis-à-vis, fourteen months after the end, showed that this was an exceptional circumstance. The usual situation was that the patient would disappear and never, or rarely, be heard from again. Perhaps there would be a Christmas card, or perhaps an accidental meeting much after termination, as with Mrs. Brown. This was thought to be the ideal, treatment as a passing phase, even a forgotten phase, having served its purpose and subsided into the past, certainly not a preoccupation. The analyst sinks into the background. He is seen to be just another person. The transference dissolves, the patient is disburdened.

"There's so much to tell you," he began. "First of all, my relationship to Joan has really blossomed. I know you remember how she would hardly dare to leave the house alone. I certainly bitched about it enough. Well, it seems to be over. She's different, and we're a lot closer."

I was surprised that his termination might have affected his wife's symptom so favorably. I wondered how one could explain such a turn of fate.

As he went on to list the developments of the previous fourteen months, I was impressed, not to say stunned. Besides the disappearance of his phobias long before, there was now an improvement in the quality of his already excellent work, accompanied by a feeling of being more himself and less a compilation of the characteristics of his colleagues; a decision to study guitar, an old ambition never acted upon; the decision to shop for a vacation home; a heightened awareness of unconscious forces at work in all relationships; some new ideas about the influence of his childhood on later development; a certain generosity entering into relationships with a wide circle of people, in and out of his immediate family. All this was taking place in the context of grief, which lent it a convincing quality, and differentiated it from a manic flight into health, a defensive response to loss. He wanted me to know all this, and along with it, the gratitude he felt for what I had done for him. I listened patiently, without interrupting, aware of the ongoing effect of long years spent listening to him.

I knew that I did not have access to details in the way one does with patients in treatment, so that my judgments about the meaning of these changes would have to be based on less than the fullest information. What he told me came as a surprise because I had not thought so highly of the work we had done. It was quite uneven, without a sense of completion. It had been a struggle from the first phone conversation and the first hour, when he began by questioning me about myself, and had continued so right through to the end.

In the final year, I had been preoccupied with the idea of putting a good face on it, and wondering whether this was the sheerest hypocrisy or some kind of ultimate wisdom. Conversations with a senior colleague long before were most pertinent to this line of thought. I had been affected by his comment that if a patient wants to interrupt treatment, it sometimes behooves the therapist to find something good about it. This was directly opposed to traditional notions of judging the wish to terminate on its merits. It resembles the response of a friend rather than a scientist. He was counteracting the analyst's usual reaction to the wish to terminate before a logical end: Analyze the resistance! I was impressed with the idea of seeing the good in an act usually thought to be hurtful. My colleague sided with the urge for independence in his patients, and was sympathetic to the view that the experience of analytic therapy was sometimes actually a hindrance to personal development. Such opinions, distinctly uncommon among people trained traditionally, drew a certain attractiveness from his having such a background. Stated by people who were trained to be eclectic, or who seemed without the rigor born of struggles for internal consistency, they could be easily dismissed.

In the matter of attitudes toward termination, similar considerations seemed to apply. When, after five and a half years, Mr. Carroll found himself with a wish to teach for a year, and a limitation on funds needed for support during that time, which might be corrected by termination of his treatment, I was ready to assent. I thought we had done as much as we could, not at all sure about how much that was. I could tell myself that his various phobias had disappeared, that he had become much more knowledgeable about himself, that he had learned to treat his wife with a greater

degree of understanding, that he had become a really generous and empathic father to his sons and daughter, and that
his dreams had gradually demonstrated a willingness to let
me understand him. Still, there was the ongoing awareness
that at some deeper level he was unwilling to be touched at
all.

During our discussions of termination, we agreed on a
six-month period leading up to it. We were arriving at the
idea that he had had successful treatment. I wasn't convinced that his treatment deserved to be regarded as wholly
successful, even with the improvements in his life. But the
very act of choosing this point of view probably contributed
to a good outcome. This may seem farfetched, but in the
light of what he told me at lunch, it wasn't at all. He needed
to feel that I regarded his efforts as successful. And I did have
a choice of viewpoints. I chose to give the most weight to
what had gone well.

I had terminated only about fifteen patients before him
who had had treatment of several years at the same frequency (four or five times a week), and my idea of what
constituted success was not fixed. One could not insist that
every patient emerge with exactly the same degree of
change toward inner coherence and growth, but what constituted an adequate result was not entirely clear. Certainly
Mr. Carroll felt that he had improved enormously, and this
had to count for a great deal.

As we sat in the restaurant, gradually becoming absorbed in conversation, progressing through the longest
lunch I had had in months, I became enthusiastic about what
he was telling me, as well as about the ease with which we
communicated. This included a certain courtesy on his part
with respect to personal questions about me, combined with
evident curiosity, which I attempted to meet with information hardly available in the analytic process. We talked about
various people in my life, my children, activities, vacation of

the previous winter, and most pertinently some ideas on analysis generally and his analysis in particular.

I had no cogent guidelines for this sort of talk, except the authority of my own analyst, who was a generously available person after my analysis was over, but who told me little of his view of my analysis. I had wanted to know much more about this. Something of the mysterious nature of the analyst was retained by me as well, and I had wanted to dispel it, wanted to grasp the merely human, understandable nature of it all.

Mr. Carroll wondered what the outcome would have been if he had been treated by someone else. There was, of course, no convincing answer to such a question. Pressing dynamics of his own would surely have organized any situation in which he was given an adequate field for self-expression. At the same time, selective attention by individual analysts with their own interests and characteristics tends to shape the material along correspondingly individual lines. The end result is always some sort of compromise among contending forces.

During lunch, my former patient repeated a theme I had heard about during his treatment. It had to do with an older person telling a lonely, depressed younger one that he deserved good things in life. He told me an anecdote about a colleague who had come from a background that was roughly similar to his. He had given the man a generous gift in return for a number of favors, telling him that he was a good person who deserved good things. The colleague had been surprised and moved by this gift and statement and had told Mr. Carroll that no one had ever said such a thing to him. My former patient believed that I had acted similarly toward him, and was trying to let me know that the effect of the treatment transcended his own life, that through him the work was affecting other people.

He had never tired of telling me about the defective or

unsuitable presents he had received from his French relatives. There were train sets that broke and were never repaired, shoddy tennis rackets that did not allow him to compete on an equal footing with others, promises never kept to get him equipment he needed for school. I knew that he was making reference to some deeper psychological matter, something defective he had been given, or something good he had not been given. In a general sense, it was love and caring, personal investment in his life. More specifically, it was a genuine relationship to parents. This says nothing about his own possible role in resisting attempts to give him what he needed, or about the complicated interaction in which he felt unloved and thereafter, resentfully, did not permit himself to be loved. Certainly his interaction with me suggested something of the latter and much was made of it during the analysis.

I thought about my attitude toward him during most of the treatment. There had been, as I've said, a certain deadness to the work almost to the end. There was a core that appeared to be inaccessible. I took alternating attitudes toward this core, thinking sometimes that it was predominantly the result of a profound schizoid withdrawal, and at others that it was more a manipulative means of inducing struggle in another person, a kind of hide-and-seek. When holding the first point of view, I thought he couldn't help himself and felt empathy for his helplessness in the face of experiences that had closed him off. In the latter instance, I interpreted with a certain strictness, as if to stave off his attempts at manipulation. This mood always gave way to the former, with progress at a snail's pace.

His brother was considerably older than myself, but the patient was an exact contemporary of my younger brother. A childhood rivalry I had had with my brother had been revived in my responses to the patient. But self-analysis of that element in the relationship did not disperse the struggle between us. Notes taken at various periods of his treatment reveal me to have been stymied and in the throes of the most intense anger. Unable to untie the conflict, I fell into long periods of boredom. Over and over I attempted to make use of these moods as indicators of my patient's state of mind, or as transference phenomena pointing to the way he saw important figures in his life. He progressed with painful slowness until one day when our relationship suddenly changed.

He had spent the first four summers of his life at a resort in New Hampshire where my family had gone as well. He had no memory for those summers. One day toward the very end he told me that he had been discussing those years with his mother, and she mentioned that she had often taken him to a certain store for ice cream. It was called Hamilton's.

Suddenly I envisioned the store. I could remember the cool air near the counter that contained the ice cream, and the excitement of choosing a flavor, and walks along the nearby lake, where sailboats drifted in the luminous evening light. I could hear the sound of laughter and see the gaggling ducks at the shore, pecking away at what remained of the ice cream cones.

The incandescence of the moment of recollection prompted me to cross the line of self-disclosure and tell him that I knew the place. His early years had coincided precisely with the period of my own memory, and it occurred to me that he and I had, as children, been in the same place at roughly the same time. Perhaps we had even seen each other. I imagined him as a little boy visiting Hamilton's.

All this partook of a wish—my own at least, and probably his too—that a bridge be made between myself as a transference figure who represented primarily deprivation, and myself as a real figure who had intersected with his actual life and now provided him with what he lacked. In this case, it was a memory for a time in life when he had none, a cure for a deficit. His persistence in the work, not to say his unflagging devotion to the hours, demonstrated above all that he judged himself to be getting something worth his while, even if the content of his opinions was that of recurrent deprivation and frustration.

Here I volunteered, without his having to ask (which he couldn't have done), a set of observations on the world of his early childhood. I told him that I knew Hamilton's well. I described the bright blue sign, which sat atop the little colonial building, and the spirit of relaxed celebration which animated the families that stopped there for an ice cream cone during a stroll.

His treatment became imbued with enthusiasm. He questioned me for further details about the ice cream shop and the surrounding area. His dreams became more comprehensible. My interpretations were suddenly inspired. The ensuing atmosphere had an element of brotherhood about it, which was closer to the condition of our ages, and farther from the chronological distance of father and son.

At this time he began to make changes in his life. The focus fell first on the relationship to certain of his peers. Whereas he had taken pains to overlook patently unethical practices on the part of one man in particular, to whom I had been so often compared, he now made it clear that he was distancing himself and condemning him. This led to turmoil and conflict in his professional life, which he bore well. He had been shedding the sense of being a mixture of the characteristics of certain of his influential colleagues, and feeling more and more an independent self. I thought that it had to do with his becoming convinced that he was receiving from me what he had never had before, and finally trusting me. My status in his life was settled. I was no longer seen as deceptive. I theorized that an identification with me supplied him with a substitute for the inadequate identification with a father. Both his biological father, about whom his mother would tell him next to nothing, and his mother's lovers were seen as useless models from whom to derive strength for himself. This was probably the first solid male identification of his life.

The enthusiasm I felt during the period of treatment that followed my disclosure was based on the changes I saw in the patient. In addition, the work resupplied me with a brightness of memory unencumbered by conflict. I was being generous to a younger-brother figure of my own, transcending rivalry. Happening toward the end of a long piece of work, in an atmosphere that allowed a relaxation of the strictness of rules, under the notion that a dissolution of transference was in order, the episode afforded a certain spontaneity and relief. I did not stop to criticize my behavior as a breach of rules. I was glad that the practical aim of making his life a better one could win out over technical ideas of anonymity as background for the encouragement of transference, and its interpretation. I could be more of a person, as could he.

As I listened to his account of the surprising developments during the fourteen-month period after the end of his treatment, I thought that surely the final phase had something vital to do with it. I did not feel that I was in a position yet to understand how what I had done could be subsumed under the heading of psychoanalysis. Should I tell myself that this man had needed more than strict analysis could supply, and that I had supplied it? Perhaps my talent lay in permitting myself to be led to such behavior at the right moment, without having to give myself reasons for it, at least at the time.

Immersed as I was in our luncheon conversation, I did not trouble myself with this. After talking about the closing phase of his treatment, I veered off into another group of ideas about the role of fiction in the treatment process. I told him about how the therapist (I myself, actually) imagines important scenes in the life of the patient, and can derive information from these scenes that exceeds what he had been given.

The patient tells a dream and the therapist imagines it. He can't know how close what he sees is to what was actually dreamed, but he can be sure that what he sees is personal, that it is different. It is efficient and summarizing to be able to collect and integrate information into some coherent structure. It provides for an economy of thought that facilitates the therapist's ability to make inferences, to derive knowledge that can be added to the patient's. In these personal constructions, furthermore, there is room for the structuring of information from both patient and therapist which is unconscious and intuitive, ready to be recognized and brought to consciousness as it is examined by the therapist.

I told him I thought that my recollection of the ice cream shop and the surrounding community amounted to an unusual addition to his childhood, based upon my own experience. The placement of the patient as a little boy in the environment of my recollection was an act of the imagination that derived unusual verisimilitude from probable fact. In remembering something good about his childhood, I had helped to dispel the overall tone of depression and loss that he had carried with him throughout his life. A major revision of his origins had flowed from a good, symbolic memory.

He listened to me, spellbound. I was once again providing him with what almost no patient ever receives. I was lending him a piece of my own reality to compensate for a deficit of his own. Was it primarily for my own benefit? I experienced his interest as a field in which to conceive, and to disclose, a reversal of the conditions of treatment, when it was I who provided the interest, and he the disclosures. Did it betoken my own lack of reconciliation with the limitations of the therapeutic experience (yes, of course), or was it a means of getting something from the patient after years of giving, his approbation for my unparalleled devotion?

How different this was from the years of distance between us. I asked myself whether this might have been
achieved without those difficult years, the long struggle, and
I thought it unlikely. I believed that I had derived my special
importance for him, and the special effect of my willingness
to talk, only because of the background of the work, only
because I knew what I knew, because we had made our way
through specific problems posed by the work itself.

"Shall we do this again?" he asked, when the moment
arrived to separate.

"Yes, I'd like to," I told him.

We set no particular time. I knew that I wanted him to
have a chance to digest what had taken place between us,
and for the moment I did not want to take any more steps
toward him. We shook hands and walked away in opposite
directions.

EPILOGUE

There is more to human struggle than even genius can encompass. All you can be taught is a set of guidelines that come to an end just where your own capacity to conceive of something unique may begin. There is no obvious access to the healing gesture, no way to imagine what's required in the absence of the struggle to master what is already known. Theory and practice provide the necessary setting for the hard-won divergent act. This is only to point out what everyone knows anyway, that the rules of psychoanalysis are limited in the living instance, as are all other schemes of psychotherapy. This hardly depreciates these rules. On the contrary, it grants the profoundest respect to a body of thought that, by its very stringency, can call forth the deepest intuitions of the helping impulse, which, with good luck, can make of insoluble conflict the beginning of a more livable life.

INDEX